JEWISH SOCIAL STUDIES MONOGRAPH SERIES
NUMBER 2

JEWISH EDUCATION IN FRANCE, 1789–1939

by Zosa Szajkowski

Edited by Tobey B. Gitelle

CONFERENCE ON JEWISH SOCIAL STUDIES

NEW YORK 1980

DISTRIBUTED BY COLUMBIA UNIVERSITY PRESS

NEW YORK AND LONDON

Foreword

It was with profound sorrow that the Editors of *Jewish Social Studies* (hereafter called *JSS*) learned of Zosa Szajkowski's untimely death soon after the acceptance of his manuscript, *Jewish Education in France, 1789–1939*, for the second number of our Monograph Series. Unfortunately, copies of some of the archival documents, particularly those relating to the Separation Law on education, that had been requested by the Editors for use as an Appendix, naturally, could not be forthcoming. Szajkowski was also unable to make further revisions or corrections in the submitted manuscript, or to approve any changes made by this editor, who diligently tried to remain true to the author's original intentions.

To give the readers of this monograph a better understanding of the situation found in 1939, and to lend credence and support to Szajkowski's material, the Editors decided to include as Appendix II a reprint of the French portion of a "Tentative List of Jewish Educational Institutions in Axis-Occupied Countries," which appeared as a Supplement to Volume 8 of *JSS* in 1946. This had been prepared by the Research Staff of the Commission on European Jewish Cultural Reconstruction, concerned with the recapture of Hitler's looted treasures throughout Europe. The Staff, under the direction of Prof. Salo W. Baron, was headed by Dr. Hannah Arendt, who was assisted by Drs. Adolf Kober and Nathan Eck.

Some of these schools, founded long before anti-Jewish legislation forced their closing, had exerted world-wide influence on all students of religion and culture. The Rabbinical Seminary of Paris, originally a yeshivah opened in Metz in 1704, was officially shuttered in 1940. This did not deter the Jews there, however, who moved underground to Clermont-Ferrand where they were able to ordain some young rabbis in 1943. Happily, the Seminary was able to reopen in Paris in 1944. Other institutions, as can be seen in Appendix II, unfortunately, did not share the same destiny. The Appendix should also be useful because it details the admissions' requirements, curricula, financing of the schools, and the backgrounds of the students, making all facets of the educational process more inclusive.

Szajkowski, prior to his death, suggested that the readers be referred to his Yiddish article, "Yidishe Fakhshuln in Frankraykh in 19tn Yorhundert" (Jewish Vocational Schools in France in the 19th Century), which was published in *YIVO-Bleter*, 42 (1962), 81–120. He felt that it would increase their appreciation of the educational system in France, since the vocational schools integrated secular and religious subjects into their curricula and also depended on Jewish philanthropy for survival as did the regular schools. Only in the twentieth century did the Franco-Jewish school system include vocational training among its general offerings.

As mentioned before, Szajkowski presented but a draft of his article. It had to be stylistically revised and even partially rewritten. An attempt was made to clarify a few obfuscations and to correct some of the more obvious typographical errors that the author never had the chance to amend. Factual material, however, has been left untouched, and the Index of Names was prepared by me without his supervision. Should readers find inaccuracies or mistakes in the present volume, we beg their indulgence.

Szajkowski's treatment fills an important lacuna in our knowledge of French Jewry, and, therefore, the Editors of *JSS* are proud to present this monograph, which we believe to be that writer's first posthumous publication, and a significant contribution to the field of Jewish Studies.

TOBEY B. GITELLE

CONTENTS

FOREWORD iii

INTRODUCTION vi

1. EARLY EFFORTS 1

Education before Founding the Consistories in 1808—1; The First
Jewish Schools—2; City Schools for Jewish Children—6; Religious
Schools and Schools for Girls—8; The Problem of Separate Jewish
Schools—9.

2. THE PHILANTHROPIC CHARACTER OF
JEWISH EDUCATION 11

Fund-Raising—11; Poverty among Pupils—12; Vocational Schools—15.

3. ORGANIZATIONAL DIFFICULTIES 17

The Lack of Centralization—17; Jewish School Leaders—18; The
Problem of Languages—19; Teachers—21; Textbooks—24.

4. HIGHER EDUCATION 27

Rabbinical Schools—27; Lycées and Schools of Higher Education—28;
Private Schools—30.

5. THE LAST HALF-CENTURY 31

The Impact of the Separation Law on Education—31; Religious
Courses—33; Education of Immigrant Children—34.

APPENDIX I 38

APPENDIX II 40

NOTES 45

INDEX OF NAMES 63

Introduction
Zosa Szajkowski: A Bio-Bibliographical Sketch

The readers of this, probably Szajkowski's first posthumous publication, may be interested in the following succinct observations on his life, which was quite stormy at times, and on his works, enormous in quantity and high in quality. Unfortunately, neither a biography nor bibliography exist. Of course, only high points in the author's career known to this writer can be offered here.

Zosa Szajkowski[1] was born on 10 January 1911 (as he relates in a brief biographical sketch) in Zaręby Kościelne (known among Jews as Zaromb), a small, poor, isolated town in Eastern Poland having a population of 5,035 Poles and 1,254 Jews in 1921.[2] His father owned an iron supply store. He studied in a *heder* (traditional religious elementary school) and, for a brief time, in a secular Yiddish-Hebrew school. His formal education was rather desultory. Following his brother Berl's precedent, he attended the Training Seminary for Teachers of the Jewish Faith in the Polish state elementary schools in Warsaw. This institution, reputedly established by the renowned rabbi and scholar, Dr. Samuel Poznański, offered free tuition, dormitory facilities, and a modest stipend to needy students. It is doubtful whether he spent more than a year there, long enough to become involved in the communist movement.

Such drastic ideological changes were not uncommon among traditional Jews, both in the streets of Warsaw and in the *shtetls*, the Jewish small towns, that were far from being frozen communities, as portrayed nowadays by their evaluators. The events that hastened the steadfast modernization of European Jewry were World War I and the ensuing Austro-German occupation, the two Russian revolutions, the pogroms, the Balfour Declaration and the British Palestine Mandate, the drive for national independence of the various nationalities, and the growing assertiveness of Polish nationalism and antisemitism.

Szajkowski left for Paris in 1927. There he worked as a furrier, a milkman, a porter in a furniture factory, and a journalist, contributing to the Yiddish communist press under several pseudonyms, including that of Szajkowski. His first books, *Etyudn tsu der geshikhte fun eingevandertn yidishn yishuv in frankraykh* (Studies in the History of the Immigrant Jewish Settlement in France) and *Di profesyonele bavegung tsvishn di yidishe arbeter in frankraykh biz 1914* (The Trade Union Movement among the Jewish Workers in France until 1914) appeared in Paris in 1936 and 1937.[3] He left the communist party in 1937. He accepted a study fellowship (*aspirantur*) for the years 1938–39 at the YIVO-Yiddish Scientific Institute, then located in Wilno, now known as YIVO Institute for Jewish Research in New York. There, according to an 8 October 1938 letter to me, his subject of research was " 'The Relations between French and Russo-Polish Jewry' (19th century)." He worked in Paris under the guidance of Elias Tcherikower, his mentor, who, with his wife, Rivka, befriended him. By 1939, however, he was also fully involved in research on earlier periods. Testimony to that was the fact that he supplied 302 out of the 637 pages of the two volume work *Yidn in Frankraykh: shtudyen un materialn* (Jews in France: Studies and Materials) (New York, YIVO, 1942), edited by Tcherikower. Its proof sheets were the only possession that the Tcherikowers managed to take with them on their hurried escape to the United States after the Fall of France.

One may surmise that their interest in history was the link between Szaj-kowski and the Tcherikowers, typical Russian-Jewish "intelligentsia" of that period. They were persons with a great sense of dedication and human warmth. It may also be fair to conclude that it was their interest in YIVO, then identified as an active Yiddishist institution, mainly Bundist-led, but with the active participation of other Yiddish secularists, lovers of Yiddish and persons interested in a new approach to Jewish studies that turned Szajkowski into a fanatical devotee of that institution. For many years he viewed YIVO as the ex-amplary synthesis of folkism, Yiddishist cultural nationalism, with more than a shade of anti-Stalinism and socialism, both reformist and revolutionary, and modern scholarship. YIVO's interest have since broadened in this country, but in its Wilno days, it concentrated on Yiddish linguistics, East European Jewry, particularly modern and contemporary, folklore and folkculture, economics and psychology, with the aim of modernizing and educating the masses always in the background.

Upon the outbreak of World War II, Szajkowski, a volunteer, fought in the French Foreign Legion, was wounded, decorated and luckily discharged.[4] He came to the United States in September 1941. Here he joined the American Army and soon after served as a paratrooper in the 82nd Airborne Division, both here and abroad.

Szajkowski's broadened scope of research on France is reflected in his con-tributions to the last-mentioned book, *Yidn in Frankraykh* (1942). They range from a work on French impressions of Polish and Russian Jews (from the fif-teenth to nineteenth centuries), studies of the Restoration, the 1848 events and the Paris Commune, as well as eighteenth century Yiddish documents. He continued his work on France upon his arrival in the United States. His articles on the "argots" of Jewish soldiers in the French army and on the Carpentras community appeared in *YIVO-Bleter* in 1942, 1943 and 1944. He also published an article in *Jewish Social Studies* in 1942 on the Alliance Israélite Universelle and East European Jewry in the 1860s.[5]

Before and during his United States army service in France and in Germany he was of great service to YIVO, managing to amass many archival materials. Upon his return to civilian life, Szajkowski became a member of the YIVO staff, as a Research Associate specializing in archival work. During his almost 38 years of association with YIVO, he "initiated, accessioned, arranged and directed the microfilming of the enormous emigration records" of several organizations in this field. He was also in charge of arranging the Tcherikower archives and those of several large American organizations. As example of such work is his "Jewish Diplomacy. Catalogue of the David Mowshowitch Collection in YIVO" (*YB*, 1966). He also participated in the YIVO-Yad Vashem documentation projects and in processing and inventorizing the Holocaust collection on France. Mention should also be made of the exhibits arranged by Szajkowski for YIVO, on its history, on the Yiddish press in the United States, on immigration, and on the Jewish child. Catalogs of these and other exhibits were published.[6]

At the time his scholarly production steadfastly multiplied. His book, *Der loshn fun di yidn in di arba kehilles fun comtat Venaissin* (The Language of the Jews in the Four Communities of the Comtat Venaissin), a valuable study in acculturation and linguistics, was published in New York in 1948. In the same year his *Antisemitizm in der frantsoyzisher arbeter bavegung fun furierizm bizn sof fun Dreyfus afere 1845–1906* (Antisemitism in the French Labor Movement from Fourierism until the End of the Dreyfus Affair, 1845–1906) appeared in New York.[7] He also published before that on the struggle against Yiddish (*YB*, 1939) and (later) on the language of the Marranos and Sephardim (*For Max Weinreich*, 1964).

Sajkowski's *Agricultural Credit and Napoleon's Anti-Jewish Decrees* appeared in New York in 1953. It was followed in 1954 by two books, *The Economic Status of the Jews in Alsace, Metz and Lorraine, 1648–1789* and *Poverty and Social Welfare among French Jews 1800–1880*. His *Autonomy and Communal Jewish Debts during the French Revolution of 1789* was published in 1959. Szajkowski's *Jews and the French Foreign Legion* (New York, 1975) presents an historical sketch of the participation of Jews in that military outfit from its inception, but concentrates on the World War II period. It contains considerble material on the shameful treatment of North African Jews by United States diplomatic and military authorities after Liberation. It is to a considerable extent autobiographical, including as it does personal data and observations. Many of his studies in French-Jewish history are scattered in periodicals and collective volumes.

Fortunately, forty-three of these, including parts of books, were reprinted in the massive collection, *The Jews and the French Revolutions of 1789, 1830 and 1848* (New York, Ktav Publishing House, 1970, 1, 161 pp.). Of these, six items are concerned with demography, including several on the Sephardim, six deal with the situation on the eve of the 1789 Revolution, and twenty-one pertain to the Revolution, including a sizable bibliography. Of the two Napoleonic items one is a Judaica-Napoleonica bibliography. There are also eight articles on the Revolutions of 1830 and 1848 and the Second Empire. The author's lengthy forty-four page introduction, a rather disjointed and obviously hurriedly-written statement, is a summary of the contents and an elucidation of some of his approaches to French and French-Jewish history; it also contains conclusions and judgments on some specific subjects, and certain sharp disagreements with other interpretations.

To judge by Szajkowski's scholarly output, his interest in American Jewry loomed next to his coverage of the French-Jewish community. Space allows but a selective sampling of themes. Among them are the seriously debated choice of support by American Jewry of either "relief" or "reconstruction" in preparation of the then anticipated post-World War I return to normalcy (*JSS*, 1970–71); communal conflict over relief policies (*YAJSS*, 1969); distribution and budgeting (*AJHQ*, 1968–69); "private" (by relatives and *landslayte*) vs. "organized" relief (*ibid.*, 1967, 1968); and relief for German Jewry (*ibid.*, 1972). He also published a rather penetrating book on the delusions of the philanthropic Jewish leadership in financing Soviet agrarian land settlements, entitled *The Mirage of American Jewish Aid in Soviet Russia 1917–1939* (1977, privately published in 75 copies).

Szajkowski left his mark, too, on the study of immigration and immigrant adjustment. Again, I will mention some themes, such as the beginnings of Jewish mass emigration to the United States; the *fusgeyers* (on foot) exodus from Rumania (1899–1903); the maltreatment of East European immigrants in transit through Germany before 1914 (*JSS*, 1942, 1951, 1977); American Jews' attitudes to German refugees, and a "reappraisal" of the *Yahudim* (earlier German immigrants and their descendants) to the East European newcomers (*AJHQ*, 1971, 1973).

His interest in ideologies was also expressed in a number of articles on the Jewish Left in the United States. Szajkowski wrote about the 1917 Hylan-Hillquit mayoralty contest in New York City (*JSS*, 1970); Jewish pro-Wilsonian socialists during World War I (*Meassef*, 1970); the American Jewish struggle against Nazism and Communism (*AJHQ*, 1970); Judah Magnes as a pacifist (*CJ*, 1968); and the impact of the 1905 Russian Revolution on American Jews (*YAJSS*, 1978). He concentrated on the politics of overseas relief, immigration and immigrant adjustment, and communism and the Left. His studies were to a large extent based on archival materials. His approach to overseas relief, an area that has so obviously been dependent on fund raising and control, official and ideological rivalries in communal representation, lead to oft justified suspicions of the professional bureaucracy. He was inclined to overlook certain pragmatic ways of getting things done, such as the need for nonsectarian distribution of Jewish relief funds on the highest level, and the use of occasional bribery and flattery without which it would have been almost impossible to distribute relief directly to Jews in many localities and sometimes countries.

Archival studies led Szajkowski to the discovery of anti-Jewish policies in the foreign relations of the United States. His article on Elihu Root's mission to Russia in 1917 (*Proceedings AAJR*, 1969), for instance, exposed proof of it. Concerned with communism's impact on Jewish life and position, and disturbed over the ever-spreading and ever-prevalent libel of an alleged Jewish-Bolshevik alliance, Szajkowski published three volumes, *Jews, Wars and Communism*. The first (1972) deals with *The Attitude of American Jews to World War I, the Russian Revolution of 1917 and Communism (1914–45)* (subtitle). The second volume is subtitled *The Impact of the 1919–20 Red Scare on American Jewish Life* (Ktav, 1974). The title of the third is *Kolchak, Jews and the American Intervention in Northern Russia and Siberia, 1918–20* (1977, privately published in 75 copies). These volumes go beyond the specifically Jewish interests, are based, to a large extent, on archival materials and expose anti-Jewish attitudes in United States foreign relief and immigration policies, particularly after the Bolshevik Revolution. In the same area are some of his other contributions in diplomatic history, such as "American Jewish Relief in Poland and Politics, 1918-23" (*Tsiyon*, 1969), the issuance of American immigration visas to Jews (*JSS*, 1974), and deportations during World War I (*AJHQ*, 1978).

Szajkowski researched the neglect and misrepresentation of the history of pogroms. His readiness to react in writing to unjustified apologetics was attested by his "A Reappraisal of Symon Petliura and Ukrainian-Jewish Relations, 1917-1921" (*JSS*, 1969). This was a lengthy critique of an article written under the same title by Taras Hunczak (*ibid.*). Szajkowski also answered the latter's reply (*JSS*, 1970). Russian antisemitism was, in Szajkowski's view, a continuous process that transcended social orders and regimes. In the following year (1971), an article on the Jews of Russia appeared in *Meassef*. Now, his two volume *An Illustrated Sourcebook of Russian Anti-Semitism 1881–1977*, based on photographs of all kinds of materials, including official documents and illustrations, will be published in 1980, with emphasis on the 1881–82 pogroms.

Szajkowski's parents, a brother and a sister were killed by the Nazis as were most of the Jews of Zaręby. He, too, was in more than one way a survivor. He objected to what he termed the commercialization of the history of the genocidal mass-murder ("Holocaust"), to the current low level of studies in it, and to prevailing popular theological speculations. His own interest in its history was expressed in scholarly publications. He reported on European Jewish *Hurban* (Destruction) research. Right after the War he published a list of maps of ghettos, concentration and partisans' camps, wrote about the Jewish press under the German occupation in Belgium and France (*YB*, 1945, 1946), and reviewed French publications and articles on France in *YB, JSS* (1947) and later *Yad Vashem Studies* (1959). An outstanding accomplishment in this area is his *Analytical Franco-Jewish Gazetteer 1939–1945 with an Introduction to Some Problems in Writing the History of the Jews in France during World War II* (New York, privately published, 1966).[8] On a more popular level, still a product of scholarly research, is his *An Illustrated Sourcebook on the Holocaust*, consisting of reproductions of materials. The first volume appeared in 1976 and the second in 1979. The third is scheduled for early publication.

Szajkowski also wrote about "internal" Jewish diplomacy, relations between Jewish leaders in different countries, as, for instance, the Alliance Israélite Universelle and other Jewries (*JSS*, 1942, 1957, 1960; *Proceedings AAJR*, 1972); the Zionist struggle at the Versailles Peace Conference (*Shivat Tsiyon*, 1956–57), the German and Allied leaders and their support of the anti-Tsarist revolutionary movement in Russia before World War I (*JSS*, 1967). He published on Germany's policy and treatment of the Polish Jews in World War I (*Proceedings AAJR*, 1966, 1967; *YBLBI*, 1964, 1965; *JQR*, 1965) and on the German Jews' demands for national rights (*JQR*, 1965). His book, *Di onhoybn fun der yidisher kolonizatsye in Argentine* (Beginnings of Jewish [Agricultural] Colonization in Argentina) appeared in Buenos Aires in 1957.

As I have stated, this summary does not exhaust Szajkowski's manifold contributions to Jewish history. He told me in 1966, for instance, that he had already published a dozen books and nearly 250 articles. This, then, can only convey, I hope, a fair idea of the great work of the historian.

Szajkowski was wedded to the study of history and it was reported that during the last years of his life, if not earlier, he resented his prime identification as an archivist. He had an insatiable passion to establish and maintain his reputation as the pioneer and expert in hitherto unexplored or neglected areas and themes and as a critic (more often than not an oral one) of others, particularly of established academicians. This may have been caused, in part, by the fact that in this age of diplomas and degrees he failed to complete his formal education, and that, except for a brief visiting position at Brandeis University, he never attained faculty status on a campus. He was very proud of the honor of a fellowship to the American Academy for Jewish Research to which he was elected in 1960. His reaction to his receipt of the 1965 Jewish Book Council of America Book Award was satisfaction with his recognition, and the modest financial reward that would cover the immediately needed typing expenses for another publication (see note 8).

Never affluent, possibly even at rare times economically comfortable, with constant pressures to cover needs for the support of his family and of funds for secretarial services, travel and defraying of publication debts, Szajkowski was always racing against time to bring his products to press and to remain financially solvent. He was reluctant to check data and supply missing volume, issue, page numbers or years, details on which editors usually insist. He had great ingenuity for locating materials, was alert to the opening of new collections and easing of restrictions, and persisted in maintaining an aura of mystery about their locations and methods of securing them. Suspicious and disappointed, he had great fear that his unpublished writings would be misused or plagiarized. He threatened to destroy them before his death and would not entrust them to anyone. This I believe was the reason for his hasty publication of several books in processed form and in limited editions at relatively low prices.

Always in search of sponsors for his publications, he would suggest subjects for research and publication and possibilities of subsidies, at the very least modest ones to defray the cost of typing, when assured of their appearance. For the past two years he sought support of a plan for a volume to contain articles by various contributors on the Russian pogroms of 1880–81, a most important theme, but hesitated before submitting the detailed project for such a major proposal lest it be plagiarized. His usual reticence disappeared in good company, where he could be a person of prominence, if not the center of conversation, and sometimes even in the company of established historians and beginners in the field of history. After a generous helping to wine, or liquor, and tasty food (before the onset of a drastic diet), he would relax, and temporarily forget his usual worries about his wife, Hannah, their son, Isaac, his status in academe, the problems of financing his projected or completed researches, and other troublesome matters. He was very concerned with the future of the Jewish people, Israel, and mankind, in view of United States foreign policy, which was bound to lead, as he saw it, to Soviet world domination. He also became a seeker of a religious faith in Judaism, at least in theory. His criticisms and stories of varied and unusual experiences, observations and encounters with people, an inexhaustible source of solid information, should have been taped. I doubt, however, whether the avid oral history interviewers considered him important or safe enough for their recordings.

Szajkowski died on 24 Elul 5738 — 26 September 1978. His funeral was attended by many academicians, co-workers, and a large number of young students. His life was a difficult but productive one. He will be remembered among the luminaries in modern Jewish historiography. May his memory be blessed.

ABRAHAM G. DUKER

NOTES

1. I wish to acknowledge my thanks to Dina Abramowicz, head librarian of the YIVO Institute of Jewish Research, for her great help. I also owe thanks to other members of the library staff, a helpful native of Szajkowski's birthplace, who prefers to remain anonymous, for valuable information about his early life, and particularly to Mr. Morris Laub, chairman of YIVO.

Szajkowski is the name by which he was generally known. He appears under it even on the meticulous catalogue cards of the Library of Congress. His real name, however, was Yehoshua (Joshua) Frydman (Polish spelling of Friedman). Zosa (pronounced Zoza) was his pet name during his very early childhood. He was known in town as Sheeyke (little Sheeye or Joshua; Polish spelling Szyjke), which he changed to Szajke, the bases for his pseudonym Zosa Szajkowski.

2. Information will be found in *L'zikhron olam: di zaromber yidn vos zaynen umgekumen al kiddush hashem, yud elul, tav shin bet* [For Eternal Memory. The Jews of Zaromb Who Perished for the Sanctification of the Name, 10th of Elul, 5642] (New York, Zaromber Relief Committee, 1947, 68 pp.). Included in it is Szajkowski's article "Destruction of Zaręby," (Yiddish), pp. 3-23, a history of the Jewish community of the town.

During his boyhood, Zaromb, located in the interbellum period in the province (*voyevodeship*) of Bialystok (now Warsaw) and the county (*powiat*) of Ostrów Mazowiecki, was a poverty-stricken town, off the main roads and railroad (Warsaw-Bialystok line). It was set afire by the retreating Russian troops in 1914. Its Jews had also been victimized by the prevailing anarchy, hostility of the Polish troops, and the acquisitiveness of the Red Army soldiers in the Polish-Soviet War (1919-20). In peacetime, Poland's economic plight, the Polish majority, and government policy contributed their shares to the impoverishment of the Jews. According to a report of the American Jewish Joint Distribution Committee (J.D.C.), 90 per cent of the town's Jewish residents required Passover relief in 1938.

3. The orthography is in the style introduced in the Soviet Union. The first book, identified on the title page as volume I, although no subsequent volume appeared, was published by the author. The second book was published by the Khaveirim Farlag Tsuzamen (Friends [Comrades?] Together Publishers).

4. See his *Jews and the French Foreign Legion* (New York, 1975); a many-sided work, it is autobiographical to a considerable extent. It tells about his fortuitous escape from Vichy France's policy of handing over captured legionnaires to the Germans or shipping them to North Africa for hard labor on road building, to fight native rebels or, at best, from treatment as criminals.

5. His articles appeared in *Jewish Social Studies* [hereafter called *JSS*], *American Jewish Historical Quarterly [AJHQ], Historia Judaica [HJ], Proceedings of the American Academy for Jewish Research [Proceedings AAJR], YIVO-Bleter [YB], Jewish Quarterly Review [JQR], Tsiyon* (Zion), *American Jewish Archives [AJA], YIVO Annual of Jewish Social Science [YAJSS], Year Book of the Leo Baeck Institute [YBLBI], Hebrew Union College Annual [HUCA], Studies in Jewish Bibliography and Booklore, Revue des Etudes Juives—Historia Judaica [REJHI], Journal of Jewish Studies, La Rasseqna Mensile di Israel, Conservative Judaism [CJ], Yad Vashem Studies, Horeb, Meassef, Heavar, Shivat Tsiyon, Proceedings of the Association for Jewish Studies,* and others. His contributions also appeared in the *Im qedenk fun Shumel Niger, olov hasholem* (In the Memory of Samuel Niger, May He Rest in Peace) *YB,* 41 (1957-58); *For Max Weinreich* (The Hague, 1964); *Abraham Weiss Jubilee Volumè* (New York, 1964).

6. For details, see "Shaike Frydman (1911-1978)," *Yedies fun YIVO—News of the YIVO,* 147 (December 1978), 5, the source of the quoted text in this paragraph.

7. His interest in French leftist antisemitism continued with articles on the St. Simonians and socialist antisemites, and on the socialists' and radicals' role in spreading antisemitism in Algeria (*JSS,* 1947, 1948).

8. His *Analytical Franco-Jewish Gazetteer 1939–1945* (New York) earned Szajkowski the "1965 Leon Jolson Award for a Book on the Nazi Holocaust." See my remarks during its presentation to him at the annual meeting of the Jewish Book Council of America, 1 June 1966, published in *Jewish Book Annual,* 24 (5727/1966-67), 221-23.

Chapter 1

Early Efforts

The history of Jewish education in France mirrors the political, social and religious trends of the Jews for that period, 1789–1939. The fifty years prior to the French Revolution showed the modification of earlier, hardened attitudes toward the Jews, but it was not until the removal of the poll-tax and permission to reside in any part of France in 1784 that their condition was truly improved. Full citizenship privileges were granted in 1791, but only with the central organization of the Jewish community into Consistories in 1808 could these be reasonably guaranteed. Full commercial freedom had to wait another decade. Equality of faith and governmental support of synagogues and rabbis was achieved in 1831. When the oath, "More Judaico," was finally abolished in 1846, the Jews in France became legally indistinguishable from other Frenchmen.

Along with natural population growth, the change in political fortunes enabled more Jews to immigrate to France, and the Jewish population in Lorraine, for instance, grew ten-fold during the period 1752–1810, as we shall see. When the population was small, and its rights more circumscribed, education was haphazard. With centralization and government support, as well as the growing interest in the importance of education spreading from Germany and Italy, the school system was vastly improved. Heretofore, this subject has been rather neglected because of the concentration of scholars on the more promising areas of Central European Jewish education. The dramatic political developments in France have already been well-documented. Now using France's rich archival resources, this lacuna can be at least partially filled.

Education before Founding the Consistories in 1808

Traditional Jewish schooling was always an integral part of communal Jewish life in France. The census of 1784 showed 19,707 Jews living in Alsace, among whom were 116 teachers (*melamdim*), 65 private teachers and 51 students of yeshivot. The 48 rabbis and assistant rabbis and the 110 cantors there also often served as teachers. According to the 1689 by-laws, compulsory education existed in the Metz community, while by 1780 two *hedarim* are known to have existed in Paris. Bordeaux had a Talmud Torah, and both a Talmud

1

Torah and a yeshivah functioned in Saint-Esprit-lès-Bayonne. Education was also compulsory in Avignon; children had to go to school until the age of 15, otherwise the parents had to pay a fine. According to the by-laws of 1558, two Avignon communal leaders were in charge of the education of poor children, which was also the case in Carpentras according to the by-laws of 1645.[1]

In many communities Jewish religious schools functioned at the beginning of the 1789 Revolution, such as that in the small community of Marseilles recorded by the end of 1791. During the Reign of Terror (1793-94) and succeeding Thermidorian reaction (1794), most religious schools were closed. Since no secular Jewish schools existed most children did not get any education at all and many of them took up peddling at an early age.[2]

A poll of the Central Consistory of 1810 listed among 46,673 Jews living in seven regional Consistories (not including the occupied countries) 1,257 children who went to school or were engaged in "useful, productive" professions; but it is impossible to say how many of these children actually went to public, modern schools. Among the 3,713 Jews of the ten departments belonging to the regional Bordeaux Consistory, 38 children were listed as pupils or as engaged in useful professions. Yet, according to a more reliable source of 1811, only 17 children and youths were then enrolled in public schools.[3]

At a very early stage in the struggle for Jewish Emancipation the question of a secular education for Jewish children was debated. In their studies on Jews presented to the Metz Academy, and published in 1788-1789, H. Grégoire, A. Thiery and the Polish Jew, Zalkind Hourwitz, all had demanded that Jewish children be accepted in public schools.[4] In the following years the question of secular schools for Jewish children was constantly argued,[5] but such schools were founded in France at a much later date than in the neighboring German States, because of the great difference between the strength and influence of the secular Jewish intellectuals in both countries. In Germany a secular Jewish group of intellectuals was active in the Haskalah (Enlightenment) movement long before 1789, but in France, such a group of very small size and influence had only just begun to make its appearance.[6] In 1821, according to the historian Léon Kahn, only thirty Jews who could be called intellectuals lived in Paris: three rabbis; twelve scholars and writers; five merchants; one lawyer; one composer; and eight army officers. A non-Jewish pamphleteer wrote that there were then only nineteen Jews, who could have been considered as secular intellectuals in the entire department of Moselle which included the city of Metz, and six of them were still students.[7] Moreover, while in some German States the non-Jewish authorities advocated the founding of secular Jewish schools, in France, as will be shown, the authorities were not too enthusiastic about such plans, since the French school system in general was then quite primitive. In Alsace the drive toward a net of public schools failed during the Revolution of 1789. In 1790, for instance, only about one-tenth of the entire population of Provence could read and write.[8]

This does not mean, however, that the Jews were intellectually less advanced than their non-Jewish neighbors. Everything depends on what should be considered as "learned" for that period. The historian, Robert Anchel, correctly noted that when the non-Jewish population was still almost completely illiterate, Jews could already read and write, "but in Hebrew." An official at the Moselle Prefecture wrote in 1818 that even the poorest Jew saved a portion of his low income in order to provide some education for his children, and that more Jews than non-Jews could read.[9] In 1808, 363 Jews family-heads of Nancy signed the declaration of Jewish names; 161 signed in French, 109 in Hebrew, 10 in both languages, 10 in Gothic characters and 78 (mostly women) made only signs. In the Upper Rhine department only 1,608 out of 10,178 signatures were in Hebrew, since most Jews were already able to sign in French. In Nantes 6 out of 11 Jews signed in French. This, however, does not prove much. Everything depends on the given community and the documents available for research. In Rimbach (Upper Rhine), 54 out of 120 Jews signed in Hebrew characters, 48 made only signs; not one signed in French and most of the 54 who signed in Hebrew could barely do so.[10]

The First Jewish Schools

The Jewish Consistory of Paris held its first meeting on 12 May 1809. Five months later, on 14 September 1809, the Consistory took the first step toward founding parochial schools by sending out a questionnaire to ascertain the number of Jewish pupils in the public schools.[11] At first the Central Consistory restricted its educational activities to the founding of modern rabbinical schools, but on 4 January 1812 the minister of education and religious affairs wrote to the Consistory that such schools were not needed because of the small number of rabbis in France. As for elementary public schools, the minister wrote, Jewish parents could send their children to the already existing schools of the non-Jewish philanthropic committees. Should the Jews, he stated, be unable to do so owing to religious principles, they should then follow the policies of the Catholics and Protestants, who organized their own schools with the help of their own welfare organizations. According to the minister, it was up to the rabbis to take charge of the religious education of the Jewish children, as it was up to the priests to do the same for Catholic children. This was not a propitious moment to disagree with official policies and the Central Consistory accepted the minister's reply as "fatherly advice" to organize schools for poor children. Indeed, on 11 November 1812, an assembly of Parisian Jews decided to organize such a school.[12]

During the First Empire the authorities disliked the idea of founding separate Jewish public schools (*écoles primaires élémentaires*) and the same policy was followed after the fall of the Napoleonic regime. An ordinance of 29 February 1816 spoke of organizing Catholic and Protestant public schools, but not Jewish ones. The members of the governmental commission on education, among them some of France's famous scholars, were shocked by a Jewish request that Jewish schools should be financed by the city-councils.[13] Jewish communities, in spite of their official character, were then barely tolerated.[14] Again, it should be noted that the French school system was organized on a solid basis as late as the July Monarchy, by a law of 28 June 1833. In 1844 Victor Considérant wrote that 28 out of 33 million Frenchmen had no education at all. Later, on 30 November 1890, Edgar Marx, president of the Bordeaux Society for the Propagation of Vocations among Jews, stated that during the Franco-Prussian War of 1870–1871 France was defeated by the teachers of Germany.[15] Thus, even during the July Monarchy, Jews were considered to be an inferior class of citizens. On 30 January 1832 the school administration of Strasbourg wrote to the Ministry of Education about the necessity of founding public schools for Jews because they were "a foreign, ignorant and dishonest colony among the educated and productive population of Alsace."[16]

In 1817 the consistorial leader, Simon Mayer Dalmbert, suggested opening a secular Jewish public school in Paris. The necessary capital of 75,000 francs was to come from the sale of 150 bonds at 500 francs each. His project, however, was not realized.[17] In the same year, on 3 August 1817 a Jewish public school was inaugurated in Bordeaux. The initiative came from the charitable society of Jewish women and during the first years almost all of about eighty pupils were children of poor families. These women got the idea for founding such a school from the published reports of a committee for the propagation of elementary education in Paris and from visits at the local Protestant school, which was opened earlier in Bordeaux. Ten Jewish children were sent to the Protestant school where they were prepared as aide-teachers (*moniteurs*) for the Jewish school.[18] It seems that in France, Jews, who were afraid of proselytism, sometimes had more confidence in Protestant than Catholic teachers, and the Bordeaux case was not an isolated one. As will be shown, the same thing happened in Paris. In the 1830s the Consistory of Marseilles complained that the Jewish children did not get any Jewish religious education at the city's schools, which were controlled by Catholic institutions. It was decided to send poor Jewish boys to the public school of the Ecole Normale and the girls to the Protestant school, where their Jewish religious education was given to them by a rabbi.[19]

The second Jewish public school was inaugurated on 1 September 1818 in Metz with fifty pupils, mostly of poor families.[20] In Paris, another such school was opened on 4 July 1819.[21] In Nancy the question of opening a school was debated as early as 1817, but only on 26 January 1820 did the Nancy Consistory decide to start one. On 14 May the first meeting of a special school committee was held; by July, forty children were already registered in the school which opened on 24 August 1820.[22]

According to a pamphlet of June 1819, Jewish public schools also existed in Marseilles, Strasbourg and Wintzenheim. Yet, according to more reliable sources, there were no Jewish public schools then in either Marseilles or Strasbourg and only a religious school (yeshivah) existed in Wintzenheim. By 1821, it was reported that secular subjects were taught in twelve public Jewish schools.[23] In time, the number of public Jewish schools rose, not without difficulties, but at least without opposition from French officials, and by 1829 there were sixty-two Jewish schools. For a short period, the number of these schools diminished: only twenty-two existed in 1837; and thirty-one with 1,627 pupils in 1841. According to *Les Archives Israélites* many Jewish parents then sent their children to Christian schools. (Interestingly enough, the number of Protestant schools also fell during these years.) In 1842 there were twenty-seven Jewish public schools in the Upper Rhine department: twenty-three with 466 pupils were consistorial schools; and four with 155 pupils were Jewish city-schools.[24]

In general there was a tendency during the 1830s and later not to hinder religious education of the non-Catholic minorities. A circular of November 1835 prescribed in detail the religious education for Jewish and Protestant children in schools with a majority of Catholic children. Earlier, by ordinance of 17 April 1832 the Royal Council of Public Education (*Conseil royal de l'instruction publique*) had established special committees to survey the Jewish schools. These were created in each of the seven regional Consistories and also in each arrondissement with a large Jewish population. The committee was to consist of between seven and twelve members (the mayor as president, the rabbi, justice of peace, police prefect and sub-prefect, among others.)[25]

The Jews thought that as members of a minority they had to do everything, including the school-system, better than their neighbors. The author of an Alsatian Jewish novel makes a member of a local board of the Jewish school say to a teacher, "Our schools should be as good as the Christian schools and even better, if only possible." Indeed much was accomplished in the field of education by both private initiative within each Jewish family and by the Jewish communities. The following is a quantitative example: In 1843 in Mulhouse, an Alsatian city of 38,400 inhabitants, there were 720 Catholic, 900 Protestant and 180 Jewish pupils, respectively, or one student per 216 inhabitants. In

1846, 1,140 Jews lived there, which meant a larger percentage of Jewish pupils.[26]

City Schools for Jewish Children

From the aforementioned, rather unsympathetic, reply sent by the minister for education in 1812 to the Central Jewish Consistory it became clear that the Jews would have to finance Jewish schools by themselves. Later, when Jews started to open public schools the government and city-councils did give some financial help, but only after prolonged interventions. Even then the funds granted were always minimal. According to an ordinance of 29 June 1819 the Consistory had the right to include school expenses in the regular consistorial budgets covered by special taxation. Such was also the instruction published on 10 August 1819 by the Central Consistory, which called upon the Jewish communities to "organize public schools in each community with a sufficient number of Jews in order to enable children of poor parents to obtain a free education." Many years later, a Parisian Jewish lawyer proudly recalled this circular, which was published fourteen years before the law of 1833 on the introduction of public schools in France and over sixty years before the law of 16 June 1881 establishing a compulsory school system.

On 16 October 1830 the government published an ordinance on the nomination of commissions to supervise Jewish public schools; nothing however was said about the financial basis for these schools. On 8 February 1831 the government recognized rabbis as public functionaries. From then on, their salaries were paid by the government. The French Jews considered this to be the final act of their full Emancipation.[27] There was some hope that the budgets of Jewish schools, too, would be taken over by the government. Earlier, on 3 December 1830, the Parisian prefect, in replying to a Jewish request for financial help for Jewish schools, said that because separate schools for each religious group were a continuation of the past regime of intolerance, separate Jewish schools could not be welcomed. Should the Jews wish to maintain their own Jewish schools in order to provide their children with a religious education, the onus would fall upon the Jewish community. This should not be seen, however, as an expression of any anti-Jewish feelings in the beginning of the liberal regime of the July Monarchy. In any case, the Paris city-council did approve a subsidy of 300 francs for Jewish schools for the year 1830 after repeated requests beginning in 1828.[28] Following the outbeak of the 1830 Revolution the Jewish community reiterated that the new regime should not and could not refuse such financial help, and a subsidy of 600 francs was granted for the year 1831.[29] Even in Bordeaux, despite friendly relations between the Jewish community and the city administration, it was not easy to obtain financial support for the Jewish school from the city.

The Jews started to request more than token subsidies; they asked that their schools become city schools (*écoles communales*) for Jewish children. On 20 August 1833 such a request was made by the Paris Consistory, but it was not granted until almost three years later, on 20 January 1836.[30] On 7 February 1843 the Ministry of Education advised the Central Consistory that eleven Alsatian Jewish schools could become city schools; however, some city councils refused to follow the Ministry's advice.[31] Although there were more Jewish communities in the Upper Rhine department than in the Lower Rhine, the Lower Rhine had more Jewish schools because it was easier to procure the status of city schools for the Jewish schools there.[32]

The policy of various central and local administrations was to make the Jews cover as many expenses as possible even after their schools became city schools. In 1842 the city council of Paris decided to construct two new buildings for Jewish schools on condition that the Jewish community would provide 20,000 of the 200,000 francs required. On 17 July 1843 the Consistory stated in a letter to the prefect that this would mean putting the Jews on a lower social level than non-Jews and would be against the spirit of Jewish Emancipation. Yet, the Consistory feared that the adminisration would entirely abandon the plan of constructing the two badly needed buildings so the 20,000 francs were paid.[33]

In places where Jews did obtain subsidies for their schools they openly thanked the government for its support. In 1835 a new Jewish school was opened in the Alsatian community of Bischheim. The old school building was so dilapidated that many parents had to keep their children at home and the Jewish community applied to the city council for a subsidy for a new building. During a public ceremony, on 7 May 1848 all the Jews, together with the children, marched to the city hall in order to express their gratitude.[34]

The situation in the community of Nancy, where two Jewish public schools with between seventy and eighty pupils had existed already in 1830, was quite different. On 2 September 1843 the Consistory decided to close the two Jewish schools and asked the parents to send their children to the general public city schools, where special courses in Jewish religion would be organized. The exact reasons for such a decision are not known. Even *Les Archives Israélites*, a periodical of a Reform tendency which often counselled Jewish parents to send their children to non-Jewish schools, criticized the decision as premature, since the consequence could be that the Jewish children of Nancy would be left without any education at all. The Catholic circles of Nancy then conducted a sharp campaign to gain influence in the school system and thereby obtain many new privileges for their private Catholic schools. It is, of course, possible that the Jews decided to close their schools in order to help the republicans strengthen their position against reactionary Catholic influence.[35]

It is worthwhile, at this point, to compare Jewish educational facilities with the schools of another religious minority. In 1868, for example, out of the ninety-two Protestant schools with 6,829 pupils in Paris only sixteen were city schools. It seems that the Protestants wanted to be more independent than the Jews. Also, their financial status was probably better than that of the Jews; 2,495 out of the 6,829 pupils paid tuition fees.[36]

Religious Schools and Schools for Girls

One can imagine that in many cases the modern French Jewish schools were at first only old-fashioned religious schools (hedarim) which included some secular subjects. Eventually, these hedarim became entirely modernized, because the trend of both the government and the Consistories in larger communities was to combat the old-fashioned hedarim. On 21 June 1821 the Royal Commission for Education wrote to the Strasbourg school authorities that the illegal Jewish schools (i.e., hedarim) should be closed. In 1821 two private hedarim still existed in Paris; one of them belonged to the widow of the religious teacher Benjamin and she was constantly in conflict with the leaders of the first modern Jewish school in Paris.[37] In 1843 there were three illegal hedarim in Metz. In the same year, in Saint-Esprit-lès-Bayonne, the pupils of the religious schools were also taught the French language and mathematics.[38]

In many cases, where the hedarim were transformed into modern schools, the old fashioned religious teachers (melamdim) were replaced by modern educated teachers.[39] The fact that modern schools were founded later in France than in Germany made it possible to avoid the sharp conflicts between the Orthodox and Reform Jews, as was the case in Germany.[40]

At first only schools for boys were opened, but then thoughts turned to the importance of education for girls. In Paris, a Jewish public school for girls was opened as early as 1822 and in Strasbourg such a school with forty-two girls was opened on 19 February 1844.[41] In other communities the schools were co-educational from the outset with only a small enrollment of girls in each school, but that situation soon changed. In 1833 in the Hellimer (Moselle) school, there were eighteen boys and only three girls. In 1843 twenty-three boys and twenty-two girls were enrolled in the Lauterbourg Jewish school; in Hatten there were twenty boys and nine girls; in Hochfelden—twenty boys and eleven girls; in Fegersheim—thirty-six boys and eighteen girls; in Brumath—nineteen boys and fourteen girls; in Dambach—thirty boys and ten girls.

The 1845 by-laws of the school for girls in Saint-Esprit-lès-Bayonne regulated the life of the girls even in their own homes. They had to rise at 6:00 A. M. (never later than 6:30), wash their hands and faces, ears and teeth, and comb their hair. Subsequently, they had to help with the housekeeping and by 8:00 A. M. they had to be in school. Every Wednesday afternoon the girls were taught handicrafts in order to prepare them for vocational schools.[42] In this respect the Jewish schools were far more advanced than the non-Jewish ones. An historian of the schools in the department of Bouches-du-Rhône noted that the education of girls was always neglected. The ordinance of 29 February 1816 which introduced the communal schools did not even mention the education of girls. Only as late as 15 March 1850 did a law introduce the public education of girls with some reservations.[43]

In the 1840s the Jewish school committees started to organize kindergartens (known also as *asiles, salles d'asile,* and *écoles maternelles*) for very young children whose parents had to work. The first such Jewish kindergarten was opened in 1842 in Metz. Fear of Catholic proselytism of very young children had forced the Jews to organize their own kindergartens. In 1846 it was noted that over sixty Jewish children were sent by their parents to a non-Jewish kindergarten in Paris where they received no Jewish education at all.[44]

The Problem of Separate Jewish Schools

After the Jews were granted Emancipation in 1791 the Jewish leader of Lorraine, Berr Isaac Berr, appealed to his co-religionists to give their children first and foremost a religious education, but also to teach them the French language; only then, he thought, would they be ready to be sent to general, non-Jewish schools. Later, many Jewish leaders insisted on following Berr's suggestions. His son, Michel Berr, a member of the Paris Jewish school committee, was against a proposal in 1819–1820 to open a Jewish high school for fear that it would separate Jews from non-Jews. Tsarphati (Olry Terquem), an extremist leader in the struggle to reform the practice of the Jewish religion, was even opposed to separate Jewish elementary schools.[45]

In 1821 the mayor of Metz, who believed that religion was the basis of education, stated that although nothing prevented the Jews from sending their children to the city schools, the Jews also had a right to have their own schools.[46] The existence of separate Jewish schools, however, was often used for anti-Jewish propaganda. In 1824 an Alsatian pamphleteer wrote that in the entire department of Upper Rhine there were only about twenty Jewish pupils in the non-Jewish elementary schools. One year later another Alsatian pamphleteer favored the idea of having Jewish teachers for Jewish children, but not in separate Jewish schools. He insisted on separating the secular education of

Jewish children from their daily life at home. In 1843, the general council
of Upper Rhine criticized the Jews' unwillingness to send their children to non-
Jewish schools;[47] but, this was not such a simple matter. In many places Christian
schools had refused to accept Jewish children; in other schools Jewish children
were persecuted or fell victim to Catholic proselytism. David Drach, the first
teacher in the Jewish school (1819) in Paris, who was himself later converted
to Catholicism, often related the story of his brother's persecution by the other
children in a non-Jewish vocational school of Strasbourg. In a petition to the
Senate, as late as 1866, the Jews of Louvigny (Moselle) protested against the
refusal of the local school to accept Jewish children.[48] Earlier, in 1844, the
Orthodox Jewish leader, Alexandre Ben-Baruch Créhange, wrote in connection
with a proposal to open a Jewish vocational school: "We do not want to isolate
ourselves. Our only desire is to avoid forgetting our sacred faith. . . . With the
help of knowledge and work we shall detroy proselytism."[49]

As already noted, the problem of Jewish schools for religious minorities
was not restricted to Jews alone. In 1806, the sub-prefect of Château-Salins
reported that not only Jews but Protestants, too, were rejected by the communal
school. The daily exercises began and finished there with Catholic prayers;
Catholic textbooks were used, and so forth. Curiously, in 1834 the Catholics
of Walentheim protested against a suggestion that they should send their
children to a school with a Protestant majority.[50]

Mention should be made that Christian children were accepted in some
Jewish schools during this period. In Bordeaux, twenty-five out of the hundred
places made available to poor children at the Jewish school (1817) were reserved for Christian children. According to a source from 1820, the Christian
children were permitted to say their prayers in this school.[51] In 1862, twelve
out of the eighteen boys at the *externat* of the Jewish vocational school of
Strasbourg were Christian.[52]

It is of importance to note that the problem of opening separate Jewish
schools was also discussed in other countries. In England, for example, Jewish
leaders were of the opinion that Jewish children should be sent to non-Jewish
schools. Still, the idea of public schools reserved for Jewish children of Whitechapel, the "ghetto" of London, was accepted as normal. In the other schools
Jewish teachers, paid by Jewish institutions, gave lessons in religious matters to
the Jewish pupils.[53]

Chapter 2
The Philanthropic Character of
Jewish Education

Fund-Raising

On 12 April 1812 the Paris Consistory decided that a Jewish school should be directed by the philanthropic society.[54] Thus, the Franco-Jewish school system from its beginning became part of a philanthropic activity for poor children. This principle became the leitmotiv of all appeals and reports of religious schools and later of secular schools.[55] At an assembly of Parisian Jews held on 11 November 1812 celebrating the establishment of a Jewish school, the discussion mainly concerned the necessity of helping poor children.[56] The director of a project to open a Jewish secondary school (lycée) in 1820 spoke of a school for "poor children who will graduate from the consistorial elementary schools."[57] Non-Jews, too, looked upon the Jewish schools as a philanthropic activity. In 1822 an Alsatian newspaper reported that in the Jewish school of Paris "poor Jewish children" were given an education that will "encourage them to choose manual work."[58] In 1826 the Jewish school in Bordeaux was reported as doing a fine job for "poor children." As the initial financial basis for the Bordeaux school, funds were collected from the wealthy Gradis and Raba families to support poor Jewish pupils.[59] A project of 1853 to open a school preparatory to the rabbinical institution in Metz and a vocational school as well was also inspired by the desire to aid poor Jewish boys.[60] Philanthropy was also the tendency at a much later period. After the separation of Church and state, the by-laws of the society which was founded in 1905 for Jewish schools, contained a passage about "educating the poor children, including those of immigrant parents."[61]

This was in line with the social philosophy of the leaders of the Jewish communities and schools. In 1791, Berr Isaac Berr appealed for the organization of "philanthropic factories" for poor children and all those "who were not born for a higher status." In 1826 the Paris Consistory had rejected a proposal to open a lycée, since it was believed that only children of wealthy families should obtain a higher education while vocational schools would be sufficient for the poor. A higher education could only turn the Jewish worker into an unsatisfied, bitter man. Such was then the general trend in France, Germany and other countries. All this had a great influence upon the curriculum, the

attitude toward the children and their parents, and so forth. In 1843 Samuel
Cahen, editor of *Les Archives Israélites* wrote that poor Jewish children should
not learn Hebrew since they lacked the time and, therefore, they should pray
in French. Hebrew should be reserved for students of Hebrew literature.[62]

Wealthy Jews avoided sending their children to Jewish schools where there
was an institutionally philanthropic atmosphere. Drach noted in a report of
1819: "The heads of wealthy families who thought of sending their children
[to the Jewish school] had changed their minds."[63] Many Jews considered such
an attitude as quite natural; some simply resigned themselves to accept it,[64]
while other Jewish leaders warned against such a position. In 1855 *L'Univers
Israélite* complained that poor children were sent to Jewish schools and wealthy
children to Christian schools. In 1872 Alexandre Weill, a well-known Franco-
Jewish writer with many eccentric ideas, wrote that the Jewish community was
in need of a lycée not only for the poor, but also for children of all social classes,
similar to those existent in London and Frankfort am Main.[65]

Many years later, in 1920 Rabbi Maurice Liber wrote in a report on
Jewish education that until 1881 the Jewish school activities consisted of
"philanthropy through education"; it was a school system reserved for paupers.
Little, if nearly nothing, was done for the religious education of wealthy
children. To a certain degree this was true even for the period after 1881. In
1929 the same Rabbi Liber suggested that religious courses for wealthy children
in the lycées and courses for children of poor parents in the public schools
ought to be created. The latter courses were supposed to be Jewish counter-
parts of the after-school activities in the public schools (known as *garderies*),
where the Jewish children did not get any religious education.[66]

Of course, one could cite many important later Franco-Jewish leaders who
were graduated from Jewish schools;[67] yet, unless new information comes to
light, there were almost no cases of then wealthy Jewish families sending their
children to Jewish public schools.

Poverty among the Pupils

In May 1812 fifty children of thirty-seven families were registered for the
Jewish school to be opened in Paris; most of the family heads were peddlers.[68]
It is interesting to note also that mortality and other symptoms of poverty were
greater in Jewish than non-Jewish schools.[69] Jewish children could not attend
classes regularly since they had to help out at home, mostly by peddling.
Excerpts of the daily school reports of 1820–1822 written by the teacher Drach
show:

Aaron Isaac went peddling on Sunday and Monday. After the president [of the school committee] had explained to him in touching words the advantage of education over such small gains, the pupil promised to come regularly to school, but he again went peddling. . . . Jacob David demanded to be free in the evenings because he had to work. . . . Fould had left the school in order to enter at Mr. Dupont's factory. . . . The pupil David comes to school only during 3 or 4 days weekly; during the other days he delivers meat for his father, who works in a butchery. . . . Lambert left the school because he wanted to come only in the mornings. . . . Samuel Moise, the shoemaker's boy, went peddling a few days. . . . Moïse Léon, brother of David Léon who peddles, spends most of his time on the street.[70]

In 1843 only half of the nearly one hundred Jewish children of Haguenau (Lower Rhine) went to school. In 1846 the school committee of Metz complained that some pupils, mostly those of poor families, did not attend school regularly.[71] The same complaint was made in a report from Bordeaux of February 1878. Jewish children were not the exception. According to a statement on absenteeism in fifteen schools in Bordeaux, the Jewish school was then in the fifth place, while Protestant schools occupied the twelfth and fourteenth places.[72] Paradoxically, in 1833, a school inspector reported that in the county of Féret (Upper Rhine) only the Jewish children regularly came to school; Christian children usually went to school only during the three or four winter months, when they were not needed for work in the fields.[73] Thus, it seems that Jewish parents, while poorer than their non-Jewish neighbors, actually cared more about the education of their children.

Poverty greatly influenced the school budgets. On 30 July 1820 the Jewish school committee of Nancy reported that the pupils had to be supplied with clothing; in 1821 the same committee gave financial help of three francs weekly to each pupil's family.[74] In 1858, 1,220 pupils were clad by the Jewish philanthropic committee of Paris.[75] During the school years 1874–1877, that committee distributed 449,831 free lunches to the 1,650 pupils of the nine Parisian Jewish schools (three city schools, three consistorial schools and three subsidized schools.)[76] Every year the women's committee for school canteens distributed about 150,000 lunches in five schools (143,424 meals in the school year 1904/1905; 161,594 portions in the school year 1909/1910). Only less than a half of the expenses were paid by the children (8,744 out of the 20,621 francs spent in the school year 1904/1905). During the school year 1908/1909, 60 per cent of the meals in the Zadoc Kahn school were distributed free of charge.[77] During the school year 1931/1932, 136,739 lunches were distributed by the women's committee in the five city schools where all the pupils were Jewish. A similar situation existed in Marseilles.[78]

Most parents were unable to pay tuition for their children. Of the 5,058.50 francs income in the Paris school during May–December 1819 only 33.50 came from tuition; the rest was covered by consistorial subsidies and fifty-six private donations.[79] It should be noted that in the Jewish school of Paris more was then spent proportionally on the paper, ink and pens which the pupils could not buy for themselves than in non-Jewish schools. On 27 November 1820 it was noted in the diary of this school that there was a lack of paper because according to the curriculum the pupils were using it every day instead of twice a week as in all other schools.[80]

Even more difficult was the situation in the schools where the teachers were not paid regular salaries but received only the tuition paid by the parents. In 1833, for instance, the salaries of the Jewish teachers of Alsace and Moselle were covered mainly by the school charges. As a rule, Jewish parents paid a larger tuititon for their children than non-Jews. In the Protestant schools children seldom paid more than 1/2 franc monthly, but in the Jewish school of Altkirch (Upper Rhine) the tuition was 3.50 francs monthly; in Hegenheim it was 47 1/2 centimes weekly; in Strasbourg, 1.50 francs monthly; in Colmar — from 1 to 3 francs monthly, according to the wealth of the parents and the children's age; in Bischheim tall children paid 1.40 francs and short ones only 1.20 francs; in Durmenach the tuititon was fixed according to the parents' wealth; girls paid less than boys.[81] These were all large sums for poor parents. In July 1820 the parents of thirty-two out of forty pupils in the newly founded Jewish school of Nancy were unable to pay tuition.[82] In 1834, twenty-eight out of fifty-seven pupils in Lunéville, aged between five and twelve years came from poor families. In Metz, 80 out of 115 children came from poor families (1833); in Sarreguemines, 13 out of 30 children; in Sarrebourg, 21 out of 47; in Toul, 28 out of 102. In 1851, 279 out of 1,048 pupils in 32 communities of the regional Metz Consistory came from poor families. In 1851, 674 out of the 2,364 Jewish pupils in the Upper Rhine department were unable to pay tuititon; in 1875, only 6 out of 92 pupils in Bordeaux paid tuition.[83] Meanwhile, to give an indication of total school costs, in 1864 the Jewish community of Besançon spent 400 of its 7,300 francs budget on education; in Montpellier, 500 out of 1,973 francs went toward schooling in 1863–1864.[84]

The attitude of the teachers and other school authorities toward the children was often that usually applied toward paupers. According to the 1820 by-laws of the Strasbourg school the teacher had the right to use the poor pupils for heavy duties (to take care of the fire in wintertime, to clean the building, and so forth).[85] The children were told to respect and to be grateful to the benefactors of their schools. According to the by-laws of the Bordeaux schools, on the eve of Yom Kippur the pupils had to pray on the graves of the school's financial supporters. In the Parisian schools the pupils had to recite a special prayer for their benefactors.[86] On 23 July 1877 the students of the teachers' seminary of the Alliance Israélite Universelle complained against the "barbarous" attitude of the director who had constantly reminded them of their poor origins.[87]

Vocational Schools

The history of vocational Jewish schools in France was already the subject of a separate study.[88] These schools, founded at the same time as other Jewish schools, were another expression of the philanthropic attitude in the Jewish school system. It should be noted that the curriculum of the vocational schools also contained the secular and religious subjects of the regular schools and thus should be considered as an integral part of the Jewish school system.

In 1818 the Metz Consistory stated, in connection with the founding of the first Jewish school in Metz, that teaching the children to read and write was not enough; they should also be trained to become useful citizens in society, and after being graduated from the elementary schools they should be able to work in factories.[89] On 27 May 1824, Edmond Halphen, in a report of the Parisian school, suggested adding a special class for vocational education. This would encourage the parents to send their children to factories after graduation.[90] On 6 September 1830 the Nancy Consistory advised the prefect that a "society to teach professions to poor children after graduation from the elementary school" was founded.[91] The aim of the Bayonne society for vocational training (founded in September 1850) was to work for the "poor Jewish children."[92] Some Jewish leaders considered the founding of vocational schools more important than the funding of general public schools.[93] In 1854 Gerson Lévy praised the German Jewish schools where general subjects were taught in the morning and various vocations in the afternoon.[94] In the 1850s, the French school system started to encourage more vocational training programs. Still, some Jewish leaders had warned against an exaggerated spirit of industrialization in the Jewish schools. A Jewish school inspector noted in 1860 that more importance was given to the pupil's body than to his spirit.[95] Such criticism also came from Joseph Cohen, who was an ideological adversary of the Saint-Simonian philosophy of industrialization.[96]

During the distribution of prizes at the end of each school year, Jewish leaders appealed to the children to take up "useful" professions.[97] In the reports of activities of Jewish schools the fact that former pupils were active in various professions was constantly brought to the public's attention. This was not vain self-praise. The Jewish schools did accomplish much in the field of propagating manual professions and trades among Jews. Only 8 out of 223 pupils who graduated from the school in Metz between its foundation in 1818 and September 1823 took up peddling. Between 1818 and October 1829 this school had 420 pupils. By October 1829, 100 of the pupils were still at the school, 44 went to continue their studies in other schools, 3 became students in the rabbinical school, 1 went to a music school, 117 took up various professions and 28 trades, 21 became employees, 3 became teachers, and 1 a civil servant; 50 of the students remained with their parents, 20 went back to religious schools (yeshivot), only 20 started peddling, and 12 died during that period.

Five out of the ten boys who were graduated from the Nancy school in 1822 took up vocational training.[98] The same tendency was noted in later years. During the school year 1900/1901, 107 pupils were graduated from the three consistorial schools in Paris. At the beginning of the new 1901/1902 school year, sixteen of them continued their studies in the same schools, and thirty-one took up various professions or vocational training. All the others had moved to other parts of the city and no reports of their activities were available.[99]

In some communities where no vocational schools were available, the school committees also undertook the vocational training of the children. In 1821 the school committee of Metz took care of the vocational training of seven children; and between 1818–1824 seventy-one of the graduates took up vocational training.[100] The same tendency could be observed in later years. In 1891 the introduction of vocational training in the elementary Jewish schools of Metz was suggested. It was reiterated in the beginning of the twentieth century by Rabbi Levi Meyer.[101]

In connection with the philanthropic expenses of the community, one may also refer to support extended to various types of informal education given to Jewish children. For example, the communities spent sizable funds on assistance to clubs and summer camps for Jewish youth.[102] Moreover, if for some reason Jewish children found themselves imprisoned, the communities tried to help them in various ways, including financial subsidies.[103]

Chapter 3
Organizational Difficulties

The Lack of Centralization

The Jewish schools were almost always founded by the Consistories or by special committees inspired by the Consistories. Directly or through such committees the local Consistories had control over the schools. A limited control over the entire Franco-Jewish school system was exercised by the Central Consistory which, for example, had the right to approve and reject school books.[104] In Marseilles the curriculum of the school for boys had to be approved by the regional chief rabbi, who was also president of the school committee.[105] In the communities of the regional Consistory of Metz each local administrative commission of the synagogue was also in charge of supervising its schools' activities.[106]

In spite of all this control, the Franco-Jewish school system was not centralized. This situation had left much initiative and freedom of action to local Jewish leaders; the lack of a central leadership, however, was a great disadvantage for a unified curriculum, the preparation of teachers, and so forth. Already in 1820 the Parisian Jewish leader, David Singer, insisted on organizing a central body for all Franco-Jewish elementary and vocational schools. In 1843 the same demand was made by a Jewish leader of Bordeaux. (In neighboring Belgium, where the number of Jews was much smaller than in France, a central body directed the Jewish schools and there was even a project to appoint an inspector for the Jewish schools).[107] As late as 1892 to 1906 the problem of centralizing the Jewish schools was still discussed in connection with a project to open a central Jewish children's home.

The demand for centralization of the schools often came from partisans of religious reform. David Singer, who made his demand for centralization in 1820, hoped thereby that the school would become financially independent of the Consistories and morally independent of "rabbinical tyranny." Indeed, the schools were often involved in the struggle between the Orthodox and Reform Jews. Anti-Orthodox speeches were often made in the schools.[108] In 1837, Tsarphati (Olry Terquem) accused Orthodox leaders of having a belligerent attitude toward the idea of secular Jewish schools. Yet, there were exceptions. Tsarphati himself praised the Orthodox Rabbi Mayer Lambert of Metz who helped found the Metz school; but then, the Franco-Jewish schools like the communities were never fully secular. In all these schools religious

17

matters were an integral part of the curriculum, or, if otherwise, the religious education was given through additional courses. The struggle then was only over the spirit of the religious education, Orthodox or Reform.[109]

Jewish School Leaders

During the entire nineteenth century there was not one important figure among the Franco-Jewish school leaders. This, too, was probably the result of the lack of a centralized school system. On the other hand, the lack of such centralization did not excite any Jewish educational leader to make the Jewish school problem the special subject of his interest. Yet, well-known rabbis and other Jewish leaders did belong to local school committees. Nine out of the thirty-five members of the Paris school committee founded in 1874 were still members of the same committee in 1905.[110] The banker, Michel Goudchaux, was among the founders of the Jewish school in Nancy. When his personal interest had drifted away from Jewish affairs (during the Revolution of 1848 he became minister of finance), he was also no longer interested in Jewish school activities.[111] Jonas Ennery, brother of Chief Rabbi Marchand Ennery, was a private teacher for the family of the wealthy Alsatian Jewish merchant Léon Werth for a while; later he became a teacher at the Jewish school of Strasbourg. Ennery was also the author of a textbook used in Jewish schools. During the Revolution of 1848 Ennery was elected a left-wing deputy in Lower Rhine; but even then he did not give up his interest in Jewish affairs. Owing to his opposition to Napoléon III, he was forced to escape to Belgium where he once again became a teacher, later to die there in misery.[112]

Many Jews did become important leaders in the general, non-Jewish educational system of France, a fact noted by the Saint-Simonian, Léon Halévy, in 1840. The following are but a few examples. In the 1820s, Adolphe Crémieux propagated popular education. Michel Alcan, son of a soldier during the 1789 Revolution, an autodidact and deputy during the 1848 Revolution, helped to organize educational courses for workers. Jacques Weill of Sierentz was the first Alsatian teacher to introduce agricultural courses in his school; he was decorated for his handbook on agriculture which was of great service to village teachers. For many years David Lévi-Alvarès and his two sons were the moral leaders of the French school system, though none of them had any contact with the Jewish schools. There were a few exceptions, such as the poet Eugène Manuel, co-founder of the Alliance Israélite Universelle in 1860, and a close associate of the minister of education, Jules Simon. In 1878 Manuel became inspector general of the French schools. He was also active in Jewish schools, but only in Paris and not on a national scale.[113]

It seems that those Jews who performed an important role in the French school system considered the Jewish schools as part of general philanthropic activity of a limited character. It was perfectly natural for a French Jew to become a leading figure in general and even in Jewish intellectual and/or political life without ever having gone to a Jewish school. Such, for example, were the cases of Adolphe Crémieux and Joseph Salvador, who had never learned the Hebrew alphabet.[114]

The first emancipated generation of Franco-Jewish intellectuals, scholars in the field of Jewish learning, were mostly autodidacts. This was true, for example, of Samuel Cahen, editor of *La Régénération* and *Les Archives Israélites,* and author of a much-praised translation of the Bible into French. The knowledge of these intellectuals in secular subjects came not from regular schools, but from contacts with literary salons, often in Germany. Some of them, such as Cahen and the well-known Alsatian Jewish writer, Alexandre Weill, had been pupils at the yeshivah of Frankfurt am Main. According to Weill, the twelve best pupils at the yeshivah of Frankfurt were Alsatian youths.[115] Yet, the role of the Jewish religious school in France itself should not be underestimated. The great scholar, James Darmeastater, for instance, received his first education in a primary religious school.[116]

The Problem of Languages

The founding of modern Jewish schools paralleled the fight against the use of Yiddish. According to both Reform and Orthodox leaders, the replacement of Yiddish by French was a major condition for the way toward complete Emancipation and regeneration.

The fight was a very rigorous one. In Metz, the pupils were forbidden to speak any langauge other than French. In the vocational school of Strasbourg the Friday meal, the only weekly meal with meat, was taken away from the pupils who had spoken in Yiddish. In Colmar, special supervisors were watching the children, even on the street, reminding them not to speak Yiddish. Teachers who did not know French were fired from their jobs. This happened, for example, in 1831, to the teacher, Simon Blum, of Mulhouse.[117]

Yet, Yiddish was still the language of the Jews in Alsace and neighboring departments, and to a large degree even in Paris. According to a report of May 1821 about the school in Strasbourg, Yiddish was still the language of instruction for German and even French. In Metz, too, Yiddish was the language of instruction for French. On 2 January 1837 the city Council of Sélestat adopted a resolution against the Jewish teachers for using Yiddish. In 1843 the

Alsatian inspector of schools, Chevreuse, who was compared by *Les Archives Israélites* to Adolphe Crémieux and Jan Czyński for his help given to Jewish schools, sharply attacked these schools for using the "bastard language," the "barbarous anti-national jargon."[118]

In time, Yiddish was, indeed, replaced by French and the role of the schools in this process of assimilation was considerable. Even during the First Empire the school committees were looking for French-speaking teachers.[119] More time was spent teaching French than on religious subjects. In 1819, for example, eighty minutes were spent every morning on teaching French in the Metz school. In 1820 in the Bordeaux school (where no Yiddish was spoken), five hours daily were spent on French; mathematics was taught in one hour, while Hebrew and prayer instruction took three hours. In Paris, the first eighty-five minutes every morning were devoted to French and only forty-five minutes to Hebrew and religious subjects.[120] At first, French was taught by a very simple method: Hebrew prayers were translated, word by word, into French, in the same manner as it had been done for generations in Yiddish. Many children, therefore, learned a French jargon.[121]

It should be noted that at this time the French language was hardly used by the non-Jewish population of Alsace and neighboring departments. In most schools, pupils had to pay a supplement to the teachers in order to learn French. In another part of France, in the South, the teachers had to compromise before 1870 on a Franco-Provençal amalgam. Thus, the Jews played an important pioneering role in France's struggle for the introduction of French into Alsace and neighboring departments. The Jewish minority, which considered French culture as the best way to strengthen its Emancipation, easily let itself be used for this purpose. After the German annexation of Alsace-Lorraine, about one-half of the Jewish teachers were unable to adapt themselves to the use of German as the language of instruction in this province and, thus, subsequently resigned from their positions. The Jewish minority was not the only one to propagate the French language; such a role was also played by the Protestants.[122]

The possibility of using two languages of instruction was often discussed among the Alsatian Jews. This did not mean using French and Yiddish, or Hebrew, but French and German. During the first period of the fight against Yiddish, the teachers were often forced to use German instead of Yiddish. Very often, however, the German, too, had been simply a Judeao-German.[123] The Jewish Society of Strasbourg, organized for the propagation of good books, took subscriptions in both languages, French and German.[124] Even the decision made in 1820 by the school committee of Paris to introduce Sephardic pronunciation of Hebrew was perpetrated not only to unite the Ashkenazic and Sephardic Jews and to be in line with the pronunciation used by Christian Hebraists, but also to help in the struggle against the influence of Yiddish. Many Orthodox leaders (Rabbis Michel Seligman, Emanuel Deutsch and others) were against this decision and Chief Rabbi Emanuel Deutz then removed his two sons from the Parisian school.[125]

In the Jewish schools very little attention was given to teaching Hebrew as a subject or even as a sacred language of religious learning. In Bordeaux, a special course of Hebrew had to be organized in 1843; since the religious school had been replaced by a modern one, the subject of Hebrew was completely neglected.[126] In the 1870s the parents of Jewish pupils in the general non-Jewish lycées were interested in an intense religious course and not in the teaching of Hebrew.[127] As late as 1907 it was generally accepted that Hebrew should be the basis of Jewish education. On the other hand, pupils "should not know how to speak Hebrew"; it was enough for them to read and explain the sacred texts. Théodore Reinach, member of the Parisian school committee, asked for the reduction of teaching hours in Hebrew.[128] In 1909 only three out of the thirty hours in the highest class for girls were spent on Hebrew and religious subjects; two of the thirty hours in the elementary class and four of thirty hours in each class for boys.[129] In 1911 Samuel Jehuda Hober, a former teacher at the Rishon Le-Zion colony in Palestine, ridiculed the teaching of Hebrew in France.[130]

The use of Yiddish as a language of instruction in the Jewish schools and courses was out of the question. In the 1920s the Parisian community "Ohel Jacob" of repatriated Jews used Yiddish in order to combat the influence of both Catholic missionaries and Communists among Yiddish-speaking immigrants. The Consistory protested and on 28 February 1928 it demanded that only French be spoken. It did agree later to the use of Yiddish, but only on a temporary basis.[131]

Teachers

The economic situation of Jewish teachers was often disastrous; their salaries were always low. According to a report presented by an Alsatian school inspector in 1833 the teachers were often paid with meals, every day in another pupil's home, like *yeshiva bokherim* (students of yeshivot). Conditions were so bad, that during one year six Alsatian Jewish teachers were forced to take up other professions. In 1847 a Jewish teacher named the hero of a novel on Jewish teachers as Ben Tsaroth (Son of Misery). At the end of the eighteenth and the beginning of the nineteenth centuries, the cantor of the Sephardic community in Peyrehorade was also the religious teacher; nevertheless, he still had to peddle at the local market in order to keep from starving.

Often, the modern schools were located in the teachers' homes, like the old-fashioned *hedarim*. Such was the situation in Saverne (Lower Rhine) in 1843. Frequently, the parents' complete dissatisfaction with the school system found expression through denunciation of the teachers. In 1858 the Metz teacher, L. Polack, described the non-city Jewish school in the following manner: he claimed that they were more like old-fashioned religious schools than modern schools, having no well-defined curriculum. Each parent asked the teacher for another subject for his child. Actually, the weekly portion of the Bible and the writing of Yiddish letters were the main subjects of instruction.[132]

In some schools the teachers also had to take care of the school buildings. According to projected by-laws for the Bordeaux school, the teacher would be responsible for making repairs (broken windows, and so forth) at his own expense, and also to provide the fire wood. In case of illness the teacher had to pay for a substitute teacher. Since the teacher's salary mainly came from tuition charges with an additional small subsidy from the school committee, he tried to recruit as many pupils as he could. In Paris, the collection of tuition fees by the school committee and not by the teacher was introduced only as late as 1874. The philanthropic attitude to the school problem found its expression in the attitude toward the teachers; significantly, it was poor Jews who were encouraged to take up the profession of teaching.[133]

The first modern Jewish schools followed then the accepted *mutuelle* method of teaching, with only one trained teacher for the entire school and gifted pupils at the head of each class. As already noted, in Bordeaux, Jewish pupils were prepared as teacher-aides at the Protestant school for this function.

Undoubtedly, some Jewish teachers were unusually gifted. In Paris, Samuel Cahen, the aforementioned editor of *Les Archives Israélites* since 1840, had previously been a teacher in the Jewish school for a while. The Nancy school had a teacher named Marchand Ennery, who later became Chief Rabbi of France in 1846 and, as already noted, his brother, Jonas Ennery, was a teacher in Strasbourg.[134] These were exceptions, however, and at first, most of the Jewish teachers were not well prepared for their jobs.

As early as in 1791 Berr Isaac Berr wrote about the necessity of educating modern Jewish teachers of Hebrew and French. In 1825 an Alsatian pamphleteer published a plan advocating the creation of a secular Jewish teachers' seminary. According to this project, rabbis had to be the teachers of religious subjects. In 1843 a school inspector of Metz suggested that a

Jewish teachers' seminary should be opened there. In 1855, the Central Consistory proposed that the regional Consistories contribute to the founding of such a school. This problem was still being discussed in 1907 in connection with a project for a teachers' training school at the rabbinical school of Paris.[135] Nothing, however, came from any of these proposals.

Parenthetically, one should note the existence of two such teachers' training schools of the Alliance Israélite Universelle. They were designed, however, to prepare teachers for the Alliance schools outside of France, and, therefore, are beyond the purview of this monograph.

In 1837 *La Régénération* criticized Jewish teachers for possessing much knowledge in secular matters, but having no Jewish learning at all; they knew various languages, for instance, but not Hebrew. In 1843 Rabbi J. M. Nathan of Moutzig complained that the subject of Jewish religion was absolutely neglected in the general teachers' schools where Jews, too, were preparing themselves to teach in Jewish schools. As a result, the subject of religion was left to the rabbis and, in most cases, to the cantors.[136]

Still, the influence and accomplishments of the Jewish teachers were not unimportant. The Alsatian Jewish writer, Daniel Stauben, described the Alsatian Jewish teacher as: the only French-speaking person of the community; the "intellectual"; the man with a sentiment of superiority, who knew who Voltaire was; possessed of speech full of aphorisms; familiar with the latest events; he was the man who knew everyone and also was often the local matchmaker. The value of the Jewish teacher was known even outside France. Alsatian Jewish teachers, many of whom had been pupils of Jewish schools themselves became teachers and communal leaders in Algeria. In 1856 this fact was mentioned in a petition of the Jewish community of Dutlenheim, where a modern Jewish school existed after 1834.[137] Between 1831 and 1857, seven students of the rabbinical school became teachers. Sometimes, children of teachers took up the same profession in Jewish or general schools. Such, for example, was the case of Maurice Bloch, director of the city school in Bischofsheim and author of popular studies on general educational problems. His father, Joseph Bloch, was the Jewish teacher in Colmar, later at the Bischofsheim Home for Jewish Girls in Paris. After his death, the son inherited his father's position.[138]

Were there non-Jewish teachers in Jewish schools? It seems so. According to the already-noted planned by-laws for the Bordeaux school, non-Jews were acceptable as teachers. Indeed, a non-Jew had been teaching in the school and this brought forth protests from parents who demanded his replacement by a Jewish teacher, an Ashkenazic Jew named Louis Nettre. It seems that this was so in other places, as well; the school in Marseilles had a non-Jewish teacher for some time; the school at Place des Vosges in Paris employed a non-Jewish woman as a substitute for the regular teacher, and here too, many parents resented her.[139]

Although Jews as teachers employed by general non-Jewish schools is not the subject here, two facts should be cited: as early as 1792 a Jewish Jacobin of Metz named Lazare Zay was a teacher in Strasbourg; in 1815 a Jewish teacher named Maas was fired from the private school, Le Chevalier, because of his Jewish origin. Jewish teachers were often, however, the butt of chicaneries.[140]

Textbooks

From the time of their establishment at the beginning of the nineteenth century, the Jewish schools in France had to cope with the difficult problem of providing textbooks. Inasmuch as modern Jewish schoolbooks did not exist, for a time the Jewish schools of Alsace resorted to the use of Luther's Bible and/or Catholic textbooks.[141] According to a report of 1833, two-thirds of the Jewish pupils in Wissembourg did not possess any textbooks, either because they were too poor to afford them or because of the general unavailability of such books. Salomon Ulmann, who later became Chief Rabbi of France, was so poor during his stay at the Strasbourg yeshivah of Moïse Bloch, for instance, that he could not afford to buy a grammar; so he copied one 600-pages long by hand.[142] In 1819 and in the 1820s the first Jewish textbooks were published mostly in the form of Jewish catechisms, inspired by similar books in Germany or even by earlier local Christian publications. Often such books were the product of the individual initiative of Jewish teachers, rabbis, and other authors,[143] and sometimes were intended only for the local use of one or a few communities.[144] Whenever possible, popular textbooks by non-Jewish authors were used such as, for example, Filippo Sarchi's Hebrew grammar.[145] The choice was always controlled by the Central Consistory which, in accordance with the ordinance of 25 May 1844, had supervision over all textbooks. The Orthodox protested against the Consistory's powers.[146]

On 23 October 1852 a society was founded in Paris for the propagation of books for Jewish school children (*Hevrah Thora V'emuna—Société israélite des livres moraux et religieux*). The society was directed by Adolphe Franck, Albert Cohn, Salomon Munk, and other well-known scholars. A similar society was also founded in Strasbourg (*Société des bons livres de Strasbourg*). In 1853–54 the society in Paris announced a contest for the best history of Jews until the destruction of the Second Temple. The society explained that such histories by non-Jewish authors were not suitable for use in Jewish schools and that Léon Halévy's history, for example, was too concise for children.[147]

The Franco-Jewish textbooks were a reflection of the schools and their periods. A textbook from 1853 contained chapters about desired behavior of workers, employees and servants and also about employers (how they should deport themselves, and so forth). On the other hand, in an earlier textbook of 1848 the revolutionary spirit permeated, although common to all was a maskilic tendency; they were, in effect, Jewish catechisms. An anti-Jewish pamphleteer wrote in 1824 that the first textbook for Jewish children in French suffered by being written in French; for the regions where Jews seldom spoke French, a Yiddish translation was needed. The catechisms greatly influenced the renunciation of Hebrew sacred texts, even though Chief Rabbi Salomon Ulmann stated in the introduction to his own catechism that religious texts were the best method of teaching religion.[148]

For many years only Jewish history until the destruction of the Second Temple was studied. There were no modern history textbooks. In 1823 the Jewish teacher David Drach tried to publish a history for Jewish schools, but no funds were available.[149] In 1828 the Saint-Simonian, Léon Halévy, published the aforementioned history of Jews until his time but it was too terse and fragmentary and could not be adapted for use in the schools. The books by Christian authors often contained anti-Jewish sentiments. The histories by Rabbi Lion Mayer Lambert (1840) and Jassuda Bédarride (1859) were either too fragmentary or too scholarly for public schools. In 1865 Moïse Schwab published a history of the Jews from the destruction of the Second Temple until the 1860s; and a new edition of 1895 contained events until 1883. Translations of Schwab's history were also published in Greek, Italian and Ladino; but in the schools his history was not enthusiastically accepted. In 1869 Elie Aristide Astruc, a Sephardic Jew, co-founder in 1860 of the Alliance Israélite Universelle, and later Chief Rabbi of Belgium published a short history for use in the schools, but it was criticized for its Reform tendencies.[150] In 1876 the school committee in Paris announced the publication by Théodore Reinach of a history of Jews from the destruction of the Second Temple; actually it was printed only in 1884, after the committee had promised to buy 500 copies (the fifth edition was published in 1913 and dealt with events until that year).[151] In the Parisian schools one supplementary hour was devoted to events after the destruction of the Second Temple.[152] Curiously, an 1816 prospectus of a private Jewish school in Bordeaux anticipated the study of Sephardic history after the Expulsion of 1492.[153] David Fresco's history (1898) was often used in the schools until the much later publication of Simon Dubnow's history replaced it.[154] Sometimes textbooks from abroad were used, especially German-Jewish textbooks which also contained Hebrew and French texts.[155]

When popular Jewish libraries were finally organized, Jewish students also made use of them; however, at the end of the nineteenth century a Zionist periodical complained that the Franco-Jewish schools suffered from the lack of such libraries.[156] It is, perhaps, worthwhile to note parenthetically that Jewish authors not only wrote general books for students, but that these books also often contained a definite Catholic spirit.[157]

Chapter 4

Higher Education

Rabbinical Schools

As previously mentioned, the first step of the Consistories in revolutionizing the Jewish school system was to found modern yeshivahs (rabbinical schools). The Lower Rhine Consistory, for instance, tried to organize three such yeshivot in Etendorf, Bischheim and Westhoffen. Actually, these three yeshivot had already existed and were, in effect, one yeshivah having three separate levels. The one in Westhoffen was the most advanced class for rabbinical students. In 1816 the Upper Rhine Consistory considered the idea of founding three yeshivot: in Wintzenheim, under the leadership of Rabbi Moïse Bloch; in Sierentz, under the leadership of Rabbi Jacob Ulmo; and in Soultzmatt, under the leadership of Rabbi Baruch Braunschwig. On 15 November 1820 it was decided to organize a central Rabbinical Seminary in Metz for the whole of France and in May 1821 this school was inaugurated. Still, many Jewish leaders disliked the idea of a central rabbinical school. According to a circular of 22 November 1822 the Central Consistory still favored the idea of regional rabbinical schools; but the centralized school of Metz remained. (It was later transferred to Paris). By 1860 thirty-nine out of sixty-four official rabbis in France and Algeria were graduates of this seminary. During the period 1830–1929, 259 rabbis were graduated from the seminary, most of them being either Alsatian Jews or from the neighboring departments. 45 out of the 109 graduates in July 1830–October 1859 came from the Lower Rhine, 29 from the Upper Rhine, 31 from Metz and Lorraine, and 4 from other areas. The same regional origin of French rabbis prevailed in the later years. (In 1908, thirty-four of fifty rabbis in France, Algeria, Belgium and Switzerland who were graduated from the seminary came from Alsace-Lorraine).[158]

It was impossible to avoid a conflict between the Reform and Orthodox factions over the rabbinical school. In 1852, the Parisian Society Talmud Torah was established for the purpose of opening an Orthodox rabbinical school. At first, the society collaborated with the Consistory but soon the relationship between these two bodies became hostile and the new society founded first its own synagogue and then a modern yeshivah, which was later transformed into the *Petit Séminaire,* a preparatory school for the rabbinical seminary. The necessity of such a preparatory school was felt for a long time; the Upper Rhine Consistory had demanded one as early as 1840.[159]

27

Lycées and Schools of Higher Education

Many Jewish students went to lycées and universities, all of them non-Jewish institutions. During the school year 1877/1878 there were 1,385 students at the four Colmar lycées; 190 of them (slightly more than thirteen per cent) were Jews, while the total number of Jews then was only five per cent of the general population.[160]

For many years Jews, especially professors, were not accepted in all schools. The following are but a few examples. Olinde Rodrigues, one of the leading Saint-Simonians, was not admitted to the higher teachers' school because of his Jewish origin. In 1816 Professor Abelard Servedier was refused a professorship; he left for England where he became a famous geologist. Only after the 1830 Revolution did he become a professor of mathematics in France. After the 1848 Revolution, Aron Jérôme, professor of history at the Strasbourg lycée, was transferred to Lille because of his Jewish background. The Jewish mathematics professor, Weill, was fired from his position at the Haguenau lycée. Owing to the demand by the Bishop of Luçon, Isidore Cahen was fired from his position as professor at a lycée in the very Catholic department of Vendée. In connection with both of these cases, a campaign of protest against discharging Jewish professors attracted public attention. A Strasbourg lawyer warned that after firing Jewish professors Protestants would be the next victims. Indeed, the Protestants of Bordeaux protested then against excluding Protestant professors. *L'Univers Israélite* warned against the coalition of the government and the Catholic clergy: "Rome is not located anymore in Rome, but in Paris." In 1852 Jewish and Protestant students were not accepted to the Ecole Normale which prepared professors for middle and higher schools. As late as 7 July 1881 the director of the lycée in Lunéville warned that Jews were only tolerated there.[161]

One should note that these anti-Jewish actions in the French school system and other antisemitic manifestations (e.g., the 1848 anti-Jewish riots in Alsace) restrained many young Jewish intellectuals from completely breaking with their Jewish environment. Such was the case, for example, of Isidore Cahen, who became a co-founder of the Alliance Israélite Universelle, and Eugène Manuel. The latter was not shocked when he had been asked to convert to Catholicism; he remained a Jew although he was a non-believer, but he preferred not "to replace one mistake with another one."[162]

In many lycées special religious courses were organized for Jewish students. In 1860, the lycée of Saint-Etienne demanded the local Jewish community to organize a course for the Jewish students "because religious education was the basis of our educational system." In 1873, preparations were made to find a supervisor of religious education for Jewish students at the municipal lycée in Nancy. In 1874, Rabbi Elie Aristide Astruc became such a supervisor at the well-known Parisian lycée, Louis le Grand. In the same year, a synagogue and a kosher canteen were operating in the lycée of Colmar where forty years earlier the student, Abraham Javal, had been attacked by non-Jewish students.[163]

In some private schools Jewish students were given the opportunity to receive a religious education if one of the professors happened to be Jewish. This was the case of a private school in which Professor Joseph Derenbourg taught. A few private Jewish schools even had the status of lycées. One of these, the Springer Institution, for example, was also a boarding-school and many of its students went out to non-Jewish lycées as well.[164]

There were other projects for the creation of a Jewish lycée. As already noted, in 1820, Michel Berr opposed the founding of schools for higher Jewish education fearing that this could prevent the assimilation of the future generations.[165] In the Sephardic community of Saint-Esprit-lès-Bayonne many Jewish students went to the local lycée. In 1840, a plan to open a secular lycée for students of all faiths there was proposed. The project was not realized because the Catholics insisted on appointing only Catholic professors. In 1854, Rabbi L. Marx once again tried to open a Jewish lycée, but without success. Later, in 1879, a new city lycée was opened in Saint-Esprit-lès-Bayonne in large part through the efforts of the Jewish mayor, Abraham Auguste Furtado. In the meantime, a private Jewish lycée existed for some years.[166]

In 1874, Jules Rosenfeld, a well-known social worker in the Parisian community, suggested opening a Jewish lycée patterned along the lines of the German *Realschule*. One member of the Jewish school committee opposed Rosenfeld's project contending that the basic aim of this committee was to give only primary education to children of poor families. The well-known Jewish leader, Albert Cohn, however, did approve of Rosenfeld's idea, but because of financial difficulties the project was never seriously discussed. In 1897, a group of Orthodox Jews tried to open a Jewish lycée in Paris so that the Jewish students could observe the Sabbath. Only as late as 1932 was the idea of a Jewish lycée realized. The preparatory school of the Rabbinical Seminary became a lycée under the name of Ecole Maimonide (Maimonides School), with 40 students in its first year and 180 in 1939.[167] At that time, religious courses, conducted by rabbis, existed in six Parisian lycées. The participation of Jewish students was not compulsory.[168] Organizations of Jewish university students first came into being in the 1880s–1890s among the immigrant students from Eastern Europe.[169]

Educational courses for adults are not within the scope of the present study, although a few facts should be mentioned. The groups of elderly Jews mostly met for religious learning. In Paris, Hebrew courses existed in the 1840s. In Carpentras, elderly Jews learned religious texts every Saturday at the house of the merchant, Elias Valabrègue. (In 1848, the cantor of Carpentras issued an appeal for the religious education of children). In 1896, a society for the propagation of Jewish knowledge existed in Bayonne. In Mulhouse, a similar group of elderly Jews met in the 1920s.[170]

Private Schools

Before the Emancipation, wealthy Jews had retained private religious teachers (*melamdim*) for their children, while after the Emancipation, many wealthy Jews hired private teachers for secular subjects. In 1834, 25 of the 340 Jewish children who received an education in Metz had private teachers. There were also many private Jewish schools with a mixed curriculum of secular and religious subjects. In 1816, a plan to open a private Jewish school was announced in Bordeaux. In some cases such schools were only boarding-schools and the pupils were sent to other schools.[171]

The Jewish communities often sent children of poor families to private Jewish schools and paid their tuition. In 1853, the Consistory of Paris sent 100 children to private Jewish schools and two years later 259 children. At the age of five years, the Franco-Jewish poet, Eugène Manuel, learned Hebrew in a school owned by the wife of Samuel Cahen, editor of *Les Archives Israélites*. In 1858, three private Jewish schools existed in Paris. In Metz, two private Jewish boarding-schools existed in 1826, and three in 1833 with 143 girls, some of them under the supervision of the philanthropic women's committee. In 1827, a private school for girls existed in Nancy and at various times such schools also existed in Strasbourg, Marseilles and Carpentras.[172]

Among the most active private Jewish schools were those of Saint-Esprit-lès-Bayonne. A few generations of pupils passed through the private school of Léon, whose curriculum consisted mainly of the French language and mathematics. An Alsatian Jewish teacher, Isidore Léon, opened a school for secular and religious subjects in this Sephardic community. In 1842, a private Jewish school for girls existed there.[173]

Chapter 5

The Last Half-Century

The Impact of the Separation Law on Education

Franco-Jewish schools suffered from the frequent changes of political regimes which finally culminated in their secularization. This problem was often discussed by Jews. Maurice Meyer, a Jewish inspector in non-Jewish schools, wrote in 1860 that secularization would be a good event.[174] Although Jews were expected to favor secularization as a means to curtail the reactionary Catholic spirit in schools, some Jews feared such legislation. Even earlier, during the Revolution of 1848, publisher Samuel Cahen expressed the opinion that secular schools would be a victory for the Orthodox against the Reform Jews; they would be free to organize their own religious schools.[175]

In 1873 the Conseil d'Etat (State Council) ruled that Jewish Consistories had a right to receive private funds for philanthropic and educational purposes. The mood against separation of Church from the state was then strong, but it soon changed. A law of 16 June 1881 introduced the principle of free and compulsory instruction. On 24 December 1881 the clergy was permitted to give religious instruction in secondary schools only with the approval of the parents.[176] Article II of a later law (28 March 1882) excluded any religious instruction and religious observance from elementary schools. Religious instruction was allowed outside the school buildings and after regular school hours. On 31 May 1882 *L'Union Scolaire*, a Paris society of former students of Jewish elementary schools, was organized for the purpose of helping Jewish schools; (in May 1898 the society had 709 members).[177]

Soon the existence of Jewish schools was endangered by an ordinance of April 1881 (approved in 1886 by the State Council) proclaiming that religious communities could not accept and administer funds for schools. The Jewish Consistory was forced to accept the new mood of the country and assured the financial basis for the philanthropic organizations and schools by transforming them into private, non-consistorial institutions, and by obtaining for them official recognition for their public use (*d'utilité publique*). A law of 1893 on the control of the finances of religious bodies further aggravated the situation.[178]

After long and stormy discussions, the law of 9 December 1905 separated Church from the state although it permitted the Catholics, Protestants, and

Jews to organize private religious bodies. Officially the Jewish leaders did not oppose the separation, but, in fact, they did not approve of it. There was a real danger that as a result of the law on separation the Jewish schools would have to close down. The new Consistories, however, reorganized as private religious bodies, were able to continue their existence and to keep the Jewish schools open.[179] In Paris a society for elementary and vocational schools was founded that continued to direct free schools. (For a time it was suggested that the Alliance Israélite Universelle should take care of Jewish education).

In some cases, rabbis preached against secularized schools, but others, more practical rabbis, suggested using the free time from secular schools to give the pupils a religious education. The anti-religious propaganda which was almost unknown previously among the Jewish young people, became stronger. "Let us defend our youth," wrote *Les Archives Israélites* in 1908.[180]

Dos pletzl (the little place) in the 4th arrondissement (district) of Paris, was inhabited by a large population of immigrant Jews. Therein, two public schools (on Place des Vosges and Rue des Hospitalières Saint-Gervais) continued to function as "Jewish" public schools (*écoles communales*) by mere accident. These schools were open to all children but were frequented mostly by Jews. The authorities had always authorized the closing of these schools on Saturdays and Jewish holidays; instead of Saturday they were open on Thursday and this policy continued even after the separation of Church and state. Religious instruction was provided after the regular hours.

At first only the antisemites protested this practice; but soon philosemites, socialists and active Dreyfusards, who were also atheists, started to protest against abrogating the law of separation. They refused to tolerate anything that prevented the assimilation of immigrants. In 1907, *L'Humanité*, organ of the Socialist party, demanded the integration of the immigrant children into the neighboring schools. On 23 November 1907, the League for Human Rights officially protested against tolerating separate Jewish schools, where the children spoke Yiddish and were served kosher lunches, and so forth. Such protests by the liberals and leftists against separate Jewish schools did not contain even a trace of antisemitism. There were many Jews among these liberals. Only a short time earlier the Dreyfusards had emerged victorious, and they were not desirous of giving the Catholics an excuse to demand separate Catholic city schools. The Paris Consistory replied that only in separate schools would Jewish immigrant children start speaking French. The calls for integration were rejected. On 17 February 1908 the government replied to the petition of the League for Human Rights that keeping these schools closed on Saturdays instead of Thursdays was not normal but also not illegal. As a result of the campaign, however, the regular faculty was forbidden to teach classes of religion. Special teachers, mostly rabbis, were to teach these classes that were held outside the school premises, often in the neighboring synagogues. The French journalist, Francisque Sarcey, wrote then that he was not only against separate religious schools but also opposed in principle to Christian or Jewish hospitals and other similar institutions. The law on separation, however, did not endanger institutions other than the schools.[181]

It should be noted that the same problem existed in different countries as well. In Austria, for example, the Socialists strongly opposed separate Jewish schools. It was part of a struggle against national Jewish autonomy, a problem that did not affect French Jews.[182]

Religious Courses

Some minute semblance of religious education in school or at home became the content of Jewishness, a sentimental remembrance of the past. The poet Eugène Manuel thus recalled the study of the Pentateuch:

> Dans le Livre où revit la Loi,
> Aux premiers jours de mon enfance,
> Ma grand-mère choisit, pour moi,
> Un court verset formant sentence.
> Je devais grandir plus heureux,
> Si je le gravais dans mon âme.
> Ce vieil usage des Hébreux,
> Elle y tenait, la sainte femme.[183]

The study of religion suffered as a result of the replacement of regular Jewish schools with supplementary religious courses. In 1890 only thirty-five children were enrolled in a course given by a Jewish youth association. According to a report of 26 December 1890, the children did not learn much because the teachers did not appear regularly.[184]

In the 1930s an attempt was made to organize religious courses in four Parisian districts not only on Thursdays and Sundays, when the schools were closed, but also after classes on all school days. The children were then given the traditional French *goûter* (a snack between lunch and dinner) in order to enable the children to do their homework first, and still have time for religious instruction. Only in the Belleville district, where newly arrived immigrants resided, however, was the experiment successful.

In 1906, soon after the separation of Church and state, only twenty religious Jewish schools existed in eight communities of France (the occupied Alsace-Lorraine not included), with fifty-six teachers, thirty-seven of them in Paris; supplementary religious courses existed in twenty-three communities. There were also four private Jewish schools.[185]

Frequently, there were not enough Jewish students to form a class. In 1902 the Jewish philanthropic committee in Paris placed orphans and other poor children from various parts of the city in foster homes of the district in order to increase the enrollment of the Jewish elementary school on Avenue de Ségur which had too few pupils. Between the two wars, the Bischofsheim vocational institution for girls could accommodate at least fifty girls, while in 1936 it had only fifteen.[186] In 1938 Paris still had three elementary schools; in 1939 only one remained, the Lucien de Hirsch school. During the 1938/1939 school year the Paris Consistory conducted twenty religious courses in thirteen of the twenty districts (with 688 children) and thirteen courses in the suburbs (with 279 children).[187]

In order to understand the character of Jewish education, the Lucien de Hirsch school should be studied. The school was closed on Saturdays. Only one hour daily was reserved for religious instruction, which included reading Hebrew, a basic knowledge of Jewish history, and mainly prayers. In the higher grades the day was concluded with the evening prayer; the children said grace after the meals. Curiously, a Communist children's organization existed in this school.[188]

Almost from their inception, the Jewish schools paid much attention in their courses to the preparation of the children, both boys and girls, for confirmation. In time this became the major part of the curriculum, though it was done superficially. In 1863 the Orthodox *L'Univers Israélite* complained that the graduates of such courses were unable to read a section of the Pentateuch. Very often even the Hebrew alphabet was unknown to them. The number of official confirmation ceremonies diminished; in Paris there were: 223 in 1901; 232 in 1902; 234 in 1903; 230 in 1904; 204 in 1905; and only 177 in 1906.[189]

Education of Immigrant Children

The mass immigration of East European Jews since 1881 created a new problem to be faced by the Jewish schools. During the school year 1897/1898 only 183 out of the 715 pupils enrolled in the schools in Paris were children of native or naturalized parents; 460 were the children of immigrants from Russia-Poland and Rumania, and the remaining 72 came from other countries. In January 1898 there were only 70 native French children among 190 who lived in a Jewish children's home in Paris. In November 1912 ninety per cent of the five hundred children in the Lucien de Hirsch school were of immigrant parents. Only thirty children of French parents were registered between 1 October 1924 and 17 June 1925.[190]

Some districts were not prepared to deal with such an influx of immigrant children. In the 18th district (Montmartre) the possibility of opening a special class for forty immigrant children was discussed. This was opposed by the Paris Consistory which considered it a hindrance to assimilation. The Chief Rabbi of Paris suggested that temporarily one should only try to put the children in public schools and to free them from Saturday instruction. In 1903 it was proposed that in some classes the curriculum should, because of immigrant children, include more hours in the instruction of the French language and fewer in other subjects. The language problem often created tragi-comic situations; grown-up children were assigned to lower classes where the desks were too small for them. Only 45 out of 137 children of three Parisian Jewish schools participating in a 1904 French test made fewer than twenty mistakes each. This did not prove that immigrant children were inferior. It was pointed out that after overcoming the initial difficulties which stemmed from the language problem they erred less than the other children.[191]

At the same time the number of pupils in Jewish schools was diminishing. In October 1915 there were 947 children in the three Parisian schools (Lucien de Hirsch, Gustave de Rothschild, and Zadoc Kahn); 863 in November 1916; 645 in October 1919; and only 342 in May 1925.[192] Unfortunately, the present stage of research does not state clearly whether French Jews moved to other districts or whether they and the immigrant Jews preferred the city schools.

After the beginning of this mass immigration the Consistory saw its role as being analogous to that performed at the beginning of the nineteenth century, when schools were needed to instill morality in the poor children. Now it became necessary to "civilize" the "little Jews," those born abroad or of immigrant parents. From this point of view, much was accomplished to smooth assimilation and to provide a token Jewish education. In the 1930s the majority of students in the rabbinical and Maimonides schools were children of immigrants.[193]

There was no question of creating Franco-Jewish public schools in the spirit of those known by the East European Jews, where Hebrew or Yiddish would be the language of instruction. By themselves, the immigrant Jews of France created a very limited educational system. Similar to the entire cultural life of these immigrants their educational system was a mirror, often a distorted one, of Eastern Europe. In a single Polish city of some 15,000 Jews more children went to religious and secular schools than in all education institutions of immigrant Jews in France. Until 1925 the cultural activities in Yiddish were conducted on a nonpolitical basis in the *Kultur Lige* (Cultural League), founded in 1922. Until 1926 only one Yiddish *Tsugabschule* (supplementary school) existed. After 1925, however, the Communists took over the control of the Cultural League and from then on Yiddish education was handled on a strictly political basis: Communist; Bundist (Socialist); and Labor Zionists (Poale Zion). The Zionists conducted their activities first in French, later in Hebrew, Yiddish and French.

On the eve of World War II six institutions for immigrant Jews from Eastern Europe existed in Paris with twelve supplementary Yiddish schools and 580 children. Six of them were of the Communist Society of Friends of Yiddish Supplementary Schools; one of the pro-Zionist Federation of Jewish Societies; two of the Bundist Workmen's Circle; one of the right-wing Labor Zionists and two of the left-wing; and one of Colonie Scolaire, a nonpolitical organization. Only in the classes of the Federation and the right-wing Labor Zionists was Hebrew included in the curriculum. Classes were held on Thursdays and Sundays, when the public schools were closed, and were conducted in a strictly political spirit. The entire educational activities were connected with the political groupings of the children: Borokhov Yugnt of the left Labor Zionists, Skif of the Bund, and the Communist Pioneers; each group had about one hundred members. Religious education was anathema in the eyes of the Communists who campaigned publicly against it. On 18 September 1927 they organized a public trial against the *heder* (religious school).

The Parisian synagogues of the immigrant Jews had sixteen *hedarim* (or Talmud Torahs) with a total of 753 children. Classes, open only for boys, were held on Thursdays and Sundays. Rarely were the teachers in the *hedarim* professionally prepared; in most *hedarim* the rabbis of the synagogues were also the teachers. Hebrew was included in the curriculum of only a few *hedarim* and Yiddish in two. In the religious circles, also, not everyone was satisfied with the educational system.[194] Even before 1914, in the Talmud Torah on Rue Charlemagne, founded in 1891, some parents demanded that Hebrew should be the language of instruction in teaching Hebrew.[195] A Talmud Torah for children of immigrant Sephardim was opened in the beginning of 1909. In July 1939 a Talmud Torah was opened in a synagogue for North African Jews.[196] The children in all these schools for immigrant Jews were not connected with the children and youth organizations of native French Jews, such as the Jewish scouts (*éclaireurs israélites de France*).

There was no unity between the immigrants and the native French Jew of the Consistories, who disliked Zionism and were shocked by the behavior of the secularists. French Jewry was used to tolerating secular Jews, some of whom even belonged to the Consistories. Until the arrival of the East European Jews, however, organized Jewish secularism was unknown in France. Many immigrant Jews, or rather their children and grandchildren, were integrated into the Franco-Jewish society, married into old-stock Franco-Jewish families, and became active Jews. Immigration served as a permanent transfusion of Judaism into the tired veins of French Jewry; but this trend was not strong enough to influence the ideologies of the native Jews, nor did it influence the Franco-Jewish educational activities.

In conclusion one should say that the Franco-Jewish community made many positive gains in the field of education despite numerous mistakes. Franco-Jewish education was a reflection of the general situation of the Jewish community. Without it, the cultural attainments of French Jewry would have been even smaller.

APPENDIX I

In 1868, 52 Jewish primary schools with 2,671 students existed in the Alsatian department of Lower Rhine. Fifty-four communities had no schools, but cantors instructed the children in religious subjects. In twenty-one communities Jewish children went to Christian schools. In 1872, under the German regime, the Lower Rhine counted 19,787 Jews in 96 schools, 54 of them primary schools and 42 religious schools, with 3,145 children and 94 teachers.[197]

In the Upper Rhine Jewish schools were organized much later than in the neighboring Lower Rhine. In 1824 an anti-Jewish pamphleteer wrote that there was not even one Jewish school there. According to one source of 1845, 25 schools with 1,013 children (6 municipal schools and 19 organized by the Jewish communities) functioned. A more reliable source noted the existence of 27 schools in 1842 with only 621 children. According to a survey of 1851 only 37 out of 62 communities had schools with a total of 2,364 pupils. One community did not have a school and from twenty-four communities there was no information. In the communities where schools existed, 222 children did not go to school. In 1857, schools with 1,862 pupils existed in only 40 of the 53 communities (including 11 municipal schools). In 1872, under the German regime, 11,290 Jews resided in 37 communities; there were then 38 schools (including 18 religious) with 1,662 pupils and 22 teachers.[198]

According to a survey of September 1833 there were fifty-two primary schools in both Alsatian departments and in Moselle; twelve schools were illegal (*clandestine*), i.e., *hedarim*. In 1872 Jews lived in 203 communities of these three departments. They had 83 Jewish primary schools and 107 religious schools (mostly courses) with 6,014 pupils and 176 teachers. After the German annexation of these departments more emphasis was laid on schools for each religious group of the population. Every religious group even had its own textbooks for teaching arithmetic.[199]

The department of Moselle played a pioneering role in Jewish education. Metz was the second community to open a Jewish school. In 1834 there were 6 municipal Jewish primary schools with 349 pupils (3 in Metz) and 5 Jewish schools with 199 children subsidized by the cities. In 25 communities 307 children went to Christian schools and took lessons in religion. In 6 communities 173 children did not go to schools.[200]

In 1923, after Alsace-Lorraine returned to France, only 17 Jewish schools with 410 children existed, more than half of them in the cities of Strasbourg and Metz. This could be explained by the emigration to other parts of France and abroad; emigration from the villages to the large cities where the interest in Jewish education was lacking; the smaller number of families with many children; and by the tendency among Jews to send their children to the lower grades of secondary schools which Jews hesitated, or were unable, to organize by themselves.[201]

In Bordeaux there were a total of 65 pupils in the 2 schools and an *asile*; 74 in 1844; 100 in 1848; and 103 in 1872. The number of Jewish pupils diminished in later years: 92 in 1875; 70 in 1878. According to the census of 1874 there were 126 pupils per thousand inhabitants. Since there were 2,454 Jews in 1851 and 2,891 in 1872, the number of pupils in Jewish schools was smaller than in the non-Jewish schools, probably, because of the fact that the Jewish schools functioned mostly for poor children. Wealthy Jews, on the other hand, sent their children to municipal or private schools.[202]

In Saint-Esprit-lès-Bayonne only five children went to secondary schools.[203] Religious schools always existed there. According to the by-laws of 22 March 1826 in the Talmud Torah for poor children instruction of French and arithmetic was to be included in the curriculum. In 1830 there were also Jewish schools in the communities Peyrehorade and Toulouse, the latter a mixture of Sephardic and Ashkenazic Jews. Since 1838 the Talmud Torah was subsidized by the municipality of Saint-Esprit-lès-Bayonne and in 1848 it became a municipal primary school for Jewish children. In 1883 it was closed and the Jewish pupils were transferred to non-Jewish municipal schools. The Consistory organized additional courses for religious matters. Rabbi Emile Lévy stated then that this was a natural separation; the separation of Church and state was welcomed there as a result of the Dreyfus affair. In 1930 the Consistory spent 426 francs of its 92,831 budget for the Talmud Torah; by 1936 the school did not exist anymore.[204]

The Consistory of Marseilles nominated two commissions in 1818 to care for general and religious education. It was decided to send the youngest children to a private school, the older children to the royal secondary school and the other, poor children, were sent to be apprentices. The budget was to be covered by a special tax of 1/1000 per cent of the wealth of the "foreign" Jews. In 1821 a Jewish school for boys was created and in 1829 a separate one for girls. After 1905 the Jewish schools were closed and religious education was given to Jewish children in a Talmud Torah created for that purpose.[205]

In the department of Vaucluse (formerly the four communities of Avignon and Comtat Venaissin) very little was done about Jewish education. For a while the women's organization of Avignon gave an "elementary education" of a vocational character to the poor children. Token religious education was provided for Jewish children of Nîmes. In Lyon a Jewish school was opened in 1839 but it was closed after the law of 1882.[206]

APPENDIX II

Tentative List of Jewish Educational
Institutions in France, c. 1939[207]

I

Jewish population in 1939: about 320,000 or 0.8% of the total population.[208] More than half were foreigners—about 50,000 were refugees from Germany and Austria, and the remainder were of Rumanian, Polish and Russian origin.

The Jewish population was mostly urban—half residing in Paris, and the others distributed in Lyons, Bordeaux, Strasbourg, Marseilles, Metz, Nancy, Lille, Toulouse and Grenoble.

II

A small minority of the Jewish children attended Jewish schools. In 1932 there were 4 Jewish elementary schools in Paris; only one survived until 1939. At the outbreak of the war there there were 3 elementary day schools, one high school (in Paris), 3 vocational boarding schools, 2 teachers' seminaries, one rabbinical seminary. To these must be added 12 *Tsugabshuln* which gave courses in Jewish subjects twice a week, 3 "popular universities," 16 *hedarim*, 2 Talmud Torahs, and a number of unregistered *yeshivot* in Strasbourg. The Central Consistory provided a number of religious courses, 13 in Paris and 13 in the suburbs. Only a fraction of the children received Jewish instruction of any kind. With the exception of the high school in Paris, founded in 1932, which enjoyed a slight increase in attendance due in the main to the immigration of Jewish families with Zionist tendencies, all Jewish educational institutions suffered a sharp decline in the 1930s.

Vocational training of Jewish children was widespread among the immigrant group. Jewish vocational schools were established by the ORT during the thirties, chiefly for Jewish refugee children from Germany. In 1939, 3 schools, comprising 113 trainees, were maintained.

III

The central Jewish organization was the Consistoire Central des Juifs de France. Membership was entirely voluntary and only a small fraction of the French Jews were members. The funds of the Consistoire were derived from donations, mainly from the Rothschild family.

The Immigrant groups were not members of the Central Consistory but maintained their own organizations, synagogues and educational facilities.

IV

All Jewish schools maintained by the Consistory and the teachers' seminaries of the Alliance Israélite Universelle were recognized by the authorities. Their final examinations and their secular program were under the supervision of the Ministry of Education. State examinations usually preceded special examinations on Jewish subjects.

The educational institutions supported by the immigrant groups had no official standing; they gave only supplementary Jewish instruction.

V

The children attending Jewish elementary schools were usually from the poorest families of the immigrant groups, served by the Rothschild welfare agencies.

The students of the teachers' seminaries came from Oriental countries and were former pupils of the Alliance schools.

Since its establishment in the early nineteenth century the students of the Rabbinical Seminary were almost exclusively from Alsace-Lorraine. After 1919, however, the immigrant group among the students increased sharply.

Jewish teachers in public schools were mostly at institutions of higher education. Jewish teachers in Jewish schools belonged to the same social strata as their pupils.

VI

1. The Jewish elementary schools maintained by the Consistory, which had a budget of 223,066 francs for educational purposes in 1938, were supervised by a special Association pour le développement de l'instruction élémentaire et professionelle, under the chairmanship of Mme. Robert de Rothschild.

Their curriculum did not differ from that of the public schools; their only Jewish feature was preparation for Bar-Mitsvah and religious instruction of one hour per day. The Jewish curriculum comprised Hebrew prayers, some Jewish history and some instruction in Bible. The same was true for the so-called *Écoles de Travail*, which were a kind of orphanage, where children attending public schools received supplementary Jewish instruction. The aim of all these schools was to provide immigrant children with an education and to introduce them to French culture.

2. The Jewish high school in Paris; see under VII B.

3. The Jewish teachers' seminaries were maintained by the Alliance Israélite Universelle, whose aim was to "work everywhere for the emancipation and the moral progress of Jews and to give efficient help to all those who suffer because of their being Jews." The first school of the Alliance was founded in Tetuan in 1862. The development of the elementary school system of the Alliance from 1911 to 1938 is shown in the Table below.

Table
Alliance Schools, 1911–38, by Geographic Distribution

Country	1911		1931		1938	
	Schools	Pupils	Schools	Pupils	Schools	Pupils
Bulgaria	2	438	1	107	1	60
Greece or European Turkey before 1914	47	17,466	8	1,910	4	1,360
Other Balkan countries	...	...	18	8,000	14	4,000
Algiers	...	...	16	2,983	16	3,244
Tunis	9	3,257	6	3,251	5	3,649
Morocco	28	4,485	38	10,296	45	15,711
Syria and Lebanon	9	1.951	10	2,818	13	3,219
Palestine	12	1,828	9	3,690	7	4,082
Egypt	8	7,024	1	264	1	191
Tripoli	2	346	1	122	1	188
Iran	11	2,416	15	4,922	15	6,376
Iraq	12	2,997	7	4,989	9	5,291
Total	140	42,208	130	43,352	131	47,371

With few exceptions these schools were not wholly maintained by the Alliance, but the subventions generally covered half of their budget. The rest came from local sources, donations and tuition fees. The schools usually had 8 grades and the graduates received the Certificat d'études primaires, which was granted them by the French consular authorities. The language of instruction was French.

4. The educational system of the immigrants.

Of the 12 *Tsugabshuln* maintained in Paris, with a total of 580 pupils, 6 were maintained by the Gezellshaft der Freinde fun Yidishe Arbeter-Tsugabshulen (Communist), one by the Fédération des Sociétés Juives, 2 by the Arbeter Ring (Bund), one by the Poale Zion, one by the Left Poale Zion, and one by the Philantropishe Gezellshaft far Fershickung far Ferien.

The schools taught Jewish subjects in Yiddish. The schools of the Fédération and the Poale Zion had Hebrew courses.

Some of the above-mentioned immigrant societies maintained so-called *Folksuniversiteten*, with courses for adults: the "university" of the Fédération des Sociétés Juives, of the Gezellshaft fun Yidishe Arbeter and of the Medem-Farband (another branch of the Bundists). The language of instruction in these adult courses was Yiddish.

5. The great majority of the Orthodox Jews in France were also immigrants. They maintained some 16 *hedarim* and Talmud Torah schools which may be likened to the *Tsugabshuln* except that instruction was along strictly Orthodox religious lines. They had a total attendance of 755 pupils throughout the country. Most of these institutions were located in Paris. One Talmud Torah under the supervision of the local chief rabbi existed in Marseilles and another in Strasbourg.

VII
A

1. École Rabbinque, Paris. 9 rue Vauquelin.
Character: Rabbinical seminary. Conservative.
Founded: In 1829 (originally a *yeshivah*, founded in 1704) in Metz; since 1859 in Paris and until 1905 subsidized by the state.
Requirements for Admission: Since 1879, high school graduation. Fellowships were granted only to persons of French nationality, 18 years of age or older and French high school graduates.
Curriculum: A six-year course in Bible, Talmud, theology, Hebrew, Jewish history and literature, French history and literature, ancient and modern literature; philosophy, Latin and Greek, Semitic and modern European languages were supplementary.
Degree: Rabbi.
Legal Status: Under the supervision of the Central Consistory of Paris. From 1831 until 1905 (separation of state and Church) the Seminary was under the control of and maintained by the state.
Finances: The building belonged to the Central Consistory. The budget, including fellowships, was covered by the Central Consistory.[209]
Background of the Students: After the 1830s all students came from Alsace-Lorraine until the detachment of these provinces from France (1871), when a serious lack of pupils prevailed. After 1880, however, Jews from these provinces again started to send their children to the Seminary. In recent years the students were mostly from immigrant families with a Yiddish-speaking background.

Number of Students: 15 in 1932; 18 in 1936; 12 in 1940. Division of cantors: 15 in 1938.
Teaching Staff: 8.
Note: Closed in 1840; reopened in fall 1944.

Teachers' Seminaries

1. École Normale Israélite Orientale, 59 rue d'Auteuil, Paris.
Character: Teachers' seminary.
Orientation: Alliance İsraélite Universelle. To train teachers for Oriental countries: "Oeuvre de régénération." "Le français et l'hébreu étroitement associés pour rendre au monde juif de l'Orient sa dignité. . . ."
Founded: In the middle of the nineteenth century. Since 1880 recognized by the state.
Requirements for Admission: Certificate of elementary school. The pupils were recruited exclusively in the Alliance schools in Africa and Oriental countries. Admission was granted after examination.
Curriculum: The same as that of the French state schools of the same type, but the faculty was exclusively chosen from teachers of college level. Religious education and good instruction in Hebrew, Arabic, Spanish. 4-year course.
Degree Granted: Brevet d'état élémentaire et supérieure.
Legal Status: Since 1918 under the close supervision of the French Ministry of Education. Supervised by the Alliance Israélite Universelle. After the state examination, a Jewish examination was given, presided over by the Chief Rabbi.
Finances: Building belonged to the Alliance. All expenses were covered by the Alliance. No tuition fees.
Background of Pupils: Gifted graduates of the Alliance schools in Africa and the Near East. All from rather poor families.
Number of Pupils: By 1937 the two teachers' seminaries (see below) had trained more than 1,800 teachers in 65 years. The attendance of both dropped from 110 in 1931 to 77 in 1935, and to 40 in 1939.
2. École Orientale Normale de Filles, 64 rue Montreuil, Versailles. Status and general program identical with that of the seminary described above, except that the girls were given some additional instruction in needlework and cooking.

B

École Maimonide, 11 rue des Abondances, Boulogne/Seine.
Character: High school. *Founded*: In 1932.
Orientation: This institution was originally a Talmud Torah affiliated with the Rabbinical Seminary and designed to prepare students for the Seminary. It was strongly conservative and assimilationist.
Requirements for Admission: 4 years of elementary school.
Curriculum: Same as in the French *Lycée*. *Degree Granted*: Baccalaureate.
Legal Status: Private school recognized by the authorities under some control of the Central Consistory.
Finances: Building rented from the Rothschilds. The budget was covered by tuition fees, subsidies from the Consistory and private donations.
Background of Pupils: Mostly from immigrant middle-class families.
Educational Qualifications of Teachers: As in all French schools of the same type.

Number of Pupils: In 1932: about 40. In 1936: about 120. In 1939: about 150 boys and 30 girls. 8 classes.

Number of Teachers: About 45 during the last year.

Note: With the outbreak of the war, the director and most of the teachers were mobilized and the school was closed. Reopened in 1945 with about 80 students.

C

1. École Lucien Hirsch, 68–70 Avenue Secretan, Paris.

Character: Elementary school for boys and girls. Conservative and assimilationist.

Requirements for Admission: Children from underprivileged families chosen in the main by the Rothschild social workers.

Curriculum: The same as in the French schools, with some religious instruction.

Legal Status: Recognized and subsidized by the municipality. Supervised by a special commission, headed by Mme. Robert de Rothschild, under the control of the Central Consistory.

Finances: Maintained by the Central Consistory, donations from the Rothschilds and some subsidies from the municipality.

Number of Pupils: About 400 boys and girls in 1939. 4 classes.

2. École de Travail. 4 bis rue des Rosiers, Paris.

Character: Orphanage for boys. The children went to a French school or to École Lucien Hirsch (above). Headed by a rabbi.

Curriculum: Preparation for Bar Mitsvah, religious instruction one hour per day. Some Hebrew for prayers and some Bible.

Finances: Maintained by the Central Consistory and Rothschild donations.

3. École de Travail pour Jeunes Filles, Institution Bischoffstein, 13 Boulevard Bourdon, Neuilly/Seine.

Character: Vocational training of girls 13–18 years of age.

Requirements for Admission: Graduation from elementary school. Entrance examination.

Curriculum: The students could choose from among the following trades: elementary school teaching, commerce, needlework and tailoring, artificial flowers.

Legal Status: The institution was founded and maintained with funds donated by Mr. Bischoffstein. The administration was supervised by a *Comité des Dames* with Mme. Robert de Rothschild as chairman.

Number of Pupils: Capacity of 50 between 12 and 15 years of age. In 1936 there were only 15 pupils.

4. École de Travail. General and trade school, in Mulhouse. Similar to the preceding school.

5. École des Arts et Métiers, Strasbourg. Secular and trade school under the supervision of the Chief Rabbi of Strasbourg and under the control of the Central Consistory of Paris.

6. Jewish elementary school, in Strasbourg.

7. Jewish elementary school, in Metz.

NOTES

Abbreviations of Archival Sources

Ad — Departmental Archives

AIU — Archives of the Alliance Israélite Universelle, Paris

AN — Archives Nationales, Paris

CAHJP — Documents on education in France, at the Central Archives for the History of the Jewish People, Jerusalem

Communities — Documents of Jewish communities in France, at the Jewish Theological Seminary (JTS), New York City.

Central Consistory — Archives of the Central Consistory, Paris

Paris Consistory — Archives of the Paris Consistory

Reform — Documents on the Reform movement, at the JTS

Sephardim — Documents on the Sephardic communities, at the JTS

Tcherikower — Archives of Elias Tcherikower, at the YIVO Institute for Jewish Research, New York City

YU — Documents on education, at the Library of Yeshiva University, New York City

Abbreviations of Printed Sources

AI — *Les Archives Israélites*

EF — *La Famille de Jacob*

LI — *Le Lien d'Israël*

REJ — *Revue des Etudes Juives*

RI — *Revue Israélite*

RJL — *Revue Juive de Lorraine*

SIW — *Strassburger israelitische Wochenschrift*

UI — *L'Univers Israélite*

VI — *Vérité Israélite*

1. Gabriel Hemerdinger, "Le dénombrement des israélites d'Alsace (1784)," *REJ*, 46 (1901), 264; Charles Hoffmann, *L'Alsace au dix-huitième siècle* (Colmar, 1906), II, 17-18; Ab. Cahen, "Enseignement obligatoire édicté par la communauté israélite de Metz," *REJ*, 2 (1881), 303-305; Nathan Netter, *Vingt Siècles d'histoire d'une communauté juive. . .* (Paris, 1938), pp. 49-52; Léon Kahn, *Histoire des écoles communales et consistoires israélites de Paris* (Paris, 1884), p. 4; Louis Grimaud, *Histoire de la liberté d'enseignement en France* (Paris, 1946), VI, 289-90; Georges Cirot, *Recherches sur les Juifs espagnols et portugais à Bordeaux* (Bordeaux, 1908), pp. 74-75, 82; Henry Léon, *Histoire des Juifs de Bayonne* (Paris, 1893), pp. 363-64; Isidore Loeb, *Statuts des Juifs d'Avignon, 1779* (Versailles, 1881), p. 26; M. de Maulde, *Les Juifs dans les Etats français du Saint-Siège au moyen âge* (Paris, 1886), p. 98; Armand Mossé, *Histoire des Juifs d'Avignon et du Comtat Venaissin* (Paris, 1934), pp. 151, 169. On Carpentras rabbis who were also teachers, see Ph. Prévot, *A travers la carrière des Juifs d'Avignon* (Avignon, 5702/ 1942), pp. 34-37. For general population shifts, see Salo W. Baron, *A Social and Religious*

History of the Jews (New York, 1st. ed., 1937), II, 174.

2. *Response à de nouvelles objections pour les Sieurs Vidal et consorts. Contre les Sieurs Rigaud et consorts* (Marseilles, 1792), p. 4; Z. Szajkowski, "Jewish Religious Observance During the French Revolution of 1789," *YIVO Annual of Jewish Social Science*, 12 (1958-59), 222-24; Clément Janin, *Notice sur la communauté israëlite de Dijon* (Dijon, 1879), pp. 69-70 (in 1803 there were three Jewish teachers); A. Detcheverry, *Histoire des Israélites de Bordeaux* (Bordeaux, 1850), p. 115; Gerson-Lévy, *Considérations sur l'éducation religieuse chez les israélites anciens et modernes* (Paris, 1852), p. 9.

3. A. E. Halphen, *Recueil des lois* . . . (Paris, 1851), pp. 307-308; YU, 1-5.

4. H. Grégoire, *Essai* . . . (Paris, 1789), p. 166; M. Thiéry, *Dissertation* . . . (Paris, 1788), p. 81; Zalkind Hourwitz, *Apologie* . . . (Paris, 1789), p. 37.

5. "Depuis ma 12ème année, c'est-à-dire depuis 42 ans, je m'occupe constamment de l'instruction de la jeunesse. C'est sous mes auspices que l'école d'instruction israélite de Metz a été établie." L. M. Lambert, *Copie d'une lettre adressée à l'honorable Consistoire israélite de Metz* (Metz, 8 May 1836), 2 pp. Reform, No. 115, p. 316; Sephardim, 221-22; A. de Cologna, *Lettre d'adieu aux Israelités français* (Paris, 1826), p. 5; S. Ulmann, *Lettre pastorale* (Paris, 16 September 1863), p. 4; J. Weinberg, *Discours prononcé le 10 janvier 1859 au Temple israélite de Lyon* (Paris, 1859), p. 10.

6. Adolf Kober, "Emancipation's Impact on the Education and Vocational Training of German Jewry," *Jewish Social Studies*, 16 (1954), 15-17; Z. Szajkowski, "La vita intellettuale profana fra gli Ebrei nella Francia del XVIII secolo," *La Rassegna mensile di Israel,* 17 (1961), 122-29, 179-91.

7. Z. Szajkowski, "Conflicts between the Orthodox and Reform Jews in France," *Horev,* 14-15 (1960), 253-58; YU; Betting de Lancastel, *Considérations sur l'état des juifs* . . . (Strasbourg, 1824), pp. 71-72.

8. R. Reuss, *Notes sur l'instruction primaire en Alsace pendant la Révolution* (Paris, 1910), p. 307; August Gleize, in *Les Bouches-du-Rhône. Encyclopédie départementale,* 6 (Marseilles, 1914), 2.

9. Robert Anchel, "L'histoire des Juifs en France," *La Question juive vue par vingt-six éminentes personnalités* (Paris, 1934), p. 30; Anchel, *Napoléon et les Juifs* (Paris, 1928), p. 537; *L'Israélite français,* 2 (1818), 100-109.

10. André Gain, "La population juive de Nancy en 1808," *RJL,* 9-101 (1933), 293-94; AN, F19-11012; L. Brunschwicq, "Les Juifs de Nantes," *REJ,* 9 (1889), 305; Ad Haut-Rhin, 5E246-2.

11. Kahn, *Histoire des écoles,* p. 2.

12. YU, Lk 1, pp. 131-33, 2, pp. 128-30; Kahn, *Histoire des écoles,* pp. 2-4; Anchel, *Napoléon,* p. 541; Netter, *Vingt siècles d'histoire,* pp. 297-302.

13. Kahn, *Histoire des écoles,* pp. 1-11; S. Posener, "Establissement des écoles israélites sous l'Empire et la Restauration," *UI,* 64, Nos. 45-48 (1929), 426-29, 492-93, 527-29; Maurice Bloch, *L'Oeuvre scolaire des Juifs depuis 1789* (Paris, 1893), 27 pp., reprinted from *REJ,* 26 (1893).

14. "Notre culte était reconnu, il est vrai, mais avec toutes sortes de restrictions mentales," *La Paix,* 1847, p. 353.

15. Grimaud, *Histoire de la liberté* (1944), II, 316, 321; G. Cogniot, *La question scolaire en 1848 et la Loi Falloux* (Paris, 1948), p. 51.

16. Ad Bas-Rhin, T, Registre de corresp., écoles israélites.

17. YU, 73, Lk, p. 6; Kahn, *Histoire des écoles,* p. 6; S. Mayer Dalmbert, *Circulaire aux Israélites qui, par leurs sentiments et leur fortune, se pénétreront du devoir de concourir*

à réaliser une institution en faveur de leurs jeunes coreligionnaires (Paris, 1817), 10 pp.; second edition: *Plan d'une institution en faveur des jeunes israélites* (Paris, 1817), 12 pp.; reprinted in *L'Israélite français*, 1 (1817), 83–93.

18. Communities, 3128–31.

19. *Ibid.;* Sephardim, II, minutes of meeting, 11 May 1817. In 1830 the Protestant schools of Marseilles had 65 pupils and the Jewish 40: *Répertoire des travaux de la Société de statistique de Marseille*, 1 (1837), 113.

20. *Département du Haut-Rhin. Consistoire israélite. Circonscription de Colmar.* (Colmar, 1850), 8 pp.: "MM. les rabbins . . . organiseront . . . des cours d'instruction religieuse . . . . Extrait des registres de délibération, 17 octobre 1850."

21. *Rapport sur l'école primaire gratuité des Israélites de Paris, depuis sa fondation en mai 1819, jusqu'au 1er janvier 1820, fait au Consistoire de la circonscription et de surveillance de cette école* (Paris, 1820), 26 pp.

22. Minutes of meetings of the Nancy school (JTS); Michel Berr, *Discours prononcé le . . . 21 juillet 1827, dans une séance publique du Comité des écoles israélites de Nancy* (Nancy, n.d.), 22 pp.; S. Ulmann, *Lettre pastorale du Grand rabbin du Consistoire israélite de Nancy* (Nancy, 22 April 1844), 12 pp.; Jewish Consistory of Nancy. Sylvain May, *Rapport sur la situation du cours religieux israélite de Nancy . . . 18 décembre 1846* (Nancy, n.d.), 8 pp.; J. Libermann, *Appel du grand rabbin aux israélites de Nancy en faveur de l'école religieuse de cette ville. 11 juillet 1854* (Saint-Nicolas, 1854); *Distribution des prix faite aux élèves du cours d'instruction religieuse* (Saint-Nicolas, 1860); Jewish Consistory of Nancy . . . School Committee. *Distribution solennelle des prix . . . 20 octobre 1894* (Nancy, 1894), 13 pp.; *— 10 octobre 1895 . . .* (Nancy, 1895), 11 pp. Jewish community of Nancy. School Committee. *Distribution solennelle des prix faite aux élèves du Cours d'instruction religieuse à la synagogue le dimanche 28 décembre 1913 . . . sous la présidence de . . . Daniel Weiler* (Nancy, 1914), 16 pp.

23. *Observations du Consistoire central des Israélites, sur un imprimé adressé à Messieurs les Députés des Départements, au sujet du règlement organique, et des taxes établis pour frais du Culte mosaïque* (Paris, 22 June 1819), 11 pp.; D. Singer, *Des consistoires israélites de France* (Paris, 1820), p. 38; [E. Coquebert de Montbret], *Notice sur l'état des Israélites en France* (Paris, 1821): schools in Bergheim, Bordeaux, Haguenau, Marseilles, Metz, Nancy, Paris, Ribeauvilliers, Sarreguemines, Sierentz, Strasbourg, Thionville.

24. Grimaud, *Histoire de la liberté* (1954), VI, 144, 146; *AI*, 2 (1841), 37.

25. Royal Council of Public Instruction, *Arrêté portant qu'il sera établi des Comités spéciaux pour la surveillance des écoles primaires israélites, et contenant règlement à cet égard. Du 17 avril 1832* (Paris, May 1832), 3 pp.; Grimaud, *Histoire de la liberté*, VI, 147.

26. D. Schornstein, "Perle. Esquisses de moeurs juives en Alsace," *RI*, 3 (1872), 751; M. M. Kahan-Rabecq, *L'Alsace économique et sociale sous le règne de Louis-Philippe* (Paris, 1939), I, 282.

27. Léonce Lehmann, *Conseil d'Etat, Section de l'Intérieur. Mémoire pour le consistoire israélite de Paris* (Paris, n.d.), pp. 3–4.

28. YU, Lk 1, pp. 57, 59; Kahn, *Histoire des écoles*, p. 47.

29. Sephardim, 1041.

30. YU, Lk 1, pp. 62–64; 2, pp. 102–103; Kahn, *Histoire des écoles*, p. 52.

31. YU, 347, 452–55; *AI*, 4 (1843), 92. The eleven *écoles communales* were located in Altkirch, Durmenach, Grussenheim, Hagenthal-le-Bas, Hegenheim, Horbourg, Reguisheim, Rixheim, Sierentz, Soultzmatt, and Thann.

32. *RI*, 3 (1871), 28.

33. YU, Lk 1, p. 70; Kahn, *Histoire des écoles*, p. 57. Jewish Consistory for the District

of Paris. *A Messieurs les Membres du Consistoire central* . . . (Paris, 1846), pp. 35–36 (". . . nous nous sommes élevés avec force contre cette prétention du conseil municipal; mais il fallut nous y soumettre ou renoncer, peut-être pour toujours, à favoriser nos enfants pauvres de l'instruction primaire gratuite").

34. *Courrier du Bas-Rhin*, 27 May 1848; M. Ginsburger, *Histoire de la communauté israélite de Bischheim au Saum* (Strasbourg, 1937), pp. 116–24.

35. "Extrait des livres . . . ," *RJL*, 4–35 (1928), 88, 5–46 (1929), 91–92; *AI*, 4 (1843), 673–74; *Recueil des écrits publiés sur la question du rétablissement des écoles des Frères de la doctrine chrétienne à Nancy, en écoles communales* (Nancy, 1836), 60 pp.; P. Braun, "La Question des écoles primaires à Nancy sous le Ministère Guizot," *La Révolution de 1848*, 7 (1911), 426–33.

36. YU, 848–49.

37. YU, 447 and Lk 1, p. 17.

38. *AI*, 4 (1843), 77; YU, 190.

39. On such a case, see Schornstein, note 26 above, pp. 798–99, 811–12. For a description of *hedarim, melamdim* and teachers in an Alsatian community, see Alexandre Weill, *Ma jeunesse* . . . (Paris, 1888), pp. 34–38.

40. Charles L. Ozer, "Jewish Education in the Transition from Ghetto to Emancipation," *Historia Judaica*, 9 (1947), 75–94, 137–58.

41. *VI*, 1 (1860), 55.

42. *Règlement de l'Ecole élémentaire gratuite pour les jeunes filles israélites de St-Esprit et Bayonne* (St-Esprit, 1 January 1845), 6 pp.

43. Paul Lévy, "Les écoles juives d'Alsace et de Lorraine d'il y a un siècle," *La Tribune juive*, 15–33 (1933), 541; *AI*, 4 (1843), 280–83; A. Gleize, *Bouches-du-Rhône*, VI, 2, 8.

44. Jewish Consistory for the District of Paris, *Ecoles communales israélites de Paris. Salle d'asyle.* Paris, 10 December 1843. The Count of Rambuteau, Peer of France, Prefect of Police (Paris, 1843), 3 pp.; *Le Comité de surveillance des écoles israélites de Metz, à ses Coreligionnaires* (Metz, June 1842), 3 pp. ("D'ouvrir une école du premier âge, dit Salle d'asile, où les enfants des familles peu aisées seront reçus presqu'au sortir du berceau"). In Mulhouse such an institution was created in 1911: René Hirschler, *Les Juifs de Mulhouse* (Mulhouse, 1938), p. 14 ("Abri").

45. D. Tama, *Organisation civile et religieuse des Israélites* . . . (Paris, 1808), pp. 29–34; Michel Berr, *Observations sur un article du second volume de la Nouvelle biographie des contemporains* (Paris, 1821), p. 14. Tsarphati [Olry Terquem], *Troisième lettre d'un israélite français* . . . (Paris, 1822), p. 28.

46. *Distribution des prix faite aux élèves des écoles israélites de Metz, le 15 octobre 1921* (Metz, 1921), p. 4.

47. Betting de Lancastel, *Considérations*, p. 68; M. Tourette, *Discours sur les Juifs d'Alsace* (Strasbourg, 1825), p. 23; *Courrier du Bas-Rhin*, 12 January 1843.

48. P. L. B. Drach, *De l'harmonie entre l'Eglise et la Synagogue* . . . (Paris, 1844), I, 36; *AI*, 27 (1866), 282–83.

49. A.B.B. [Alexandre Ben-Baruch] Créhange, *Projet présenté au Consistoire central et aux consistoires des départements, pour l'établissement d'une Ecole d'arts et métiers pour les jeunes israélites* (Paris, 1844), pp. 5–6; Szajkowski, "Jewish Vocational Schools in France in the 19th Century," *YIVO-Bleter*, 42 (1962), 81–120.

50. Anchel, *Napoléon*, p. 538; AN, F17–12516.

51. ". . . l'école consistoriale de Bordeaux . . . renferme un grand nombre d'enfants

chrétiens et même ces enfants ont un local particulier où ils se retirent pour remplir les devoirs de leur religion," CAHJP, No. 5 (a letter from B. Rodrigues to the Paris Jewish school, 26 November 1820).

52. Simon Lévy, *Discours à l'inauguration du nouveau local de l'Ecole israélite des garçons* . . . (Bordeaux, 1867), p. 5. See the Jewish Consistory of the Gironde, *Inauguration du nouveau local de l'école israélite des garçons, rue Honoré Tessier* (Bordeaux, 1867); *Société d'encouragement au travail en faveur d'Israélites indigents du Bas-Rhin. . . 1863* (Strasbourg, n.d.).

53. Lloyd P. Gartner, *The Jewish Immigrant in England 1870–1914* (London, 1960), p. 229.

54. Kahn, *Histoire des écoles*, p. 5; *L'Organisation de la communauté israelité de France. Commémoration du cent-cinquantenaire de la création des Consistoires israélites par Napoléon* (Paris, 1959), p. 15, No. 64.

55. On 6 December 1815 the Bordeaux community refused two *melamdim* permission to call their *hedarim* Talmud Torahs because the parents had to pay for the instruction (Sephardim, II, p. 9).

56. "C'est donc principalement, Messieurs, sur l'éducation de la classe infortunée que doivent se porter nos regards . . . d'établir pour la classe indigente des Israélites du département de la Seine, une école gratuite," YU, Lk 2, pp. 128–30; Kahn, *Histoire des écoles*, p. 5.

57. YU, 350–60.

58. *Courrier du Bas-Rhin*, 3 January 1822.

59. ". . . les avantages que retireraient les enfants de nos pauvres de l'instruction qu'ils recevraient dans cet établissement," YU, 12, 21.

60. "Le Consistoire israélite du Haut-Rhin, justement ému de la position précaire des Israélites pauvres de notre département," *Statuts et règlements du Comité d'encouragement au travail créé à Colmar pour les jeunes gens israélites de la circonscription consistoriale du Haut-Rhin* (1853), p. 1.

61. "Association pour le développement de l'instruction élémentaire et professionnelle . . . a pour objet d'instruire les enfants pauvres; notamment ceux qui appartiennent à des familles étrangères venues s'établir définitivement en France," YU, 504; *Association pour le dévelopment de l'instruction élémentaire et professionnelle* (Paris, ca. 1906), 5 pp.; UI, 62-2 (1908), 72 ("Les écoles primaires israélites avaient été fondées pour éclairer et moraliser la classe indigente des israélites et la rendre digne du bienfait de l'émancipation").

62. Tama, *Organisation civile*, p. 34; Kahn, *Histoire des écoles*, pp. 40–41; Créhange, *Project présenté*, p. 6; *AI*, 4 (1843), 427 ("L'hébreu devrait être étudié par nos jeunes gens qui font d'autres études littéraires, mais le jeune Israélite sans fortune, destiné à manier la scie et le rabot, n'a pas assez de temps pour étudier l'hébreu. Il est vrai qu'il ne comprend pas cette langue; eh bien! qu'on permette aux ouvriers, aux femmes et à tous ceux qui ne comprennent pas la langue sainte, de prier en français").

63. YU, 257–59.

64. "Que la haute instruction, celle qui convient à la classe fortunée et celle qui est relative à la condition du peuple, ne soient ni l'une ni l'autre séparées de l'instruction religieuse." N. Noé, "Mémoire à consulter sur la réforme . . . ," Reform, 257–62.

65. *UI*, 2 (1855), 117; *RI*, 3 (1872), 466.

66. YU, 791–97.

67. Paris Consistory, minutes of meeting on education, 11 June 1929. The philosopher A. Frank was a student at the Nancy Jewish school. Léopold Kahn, a well-known publisher, was a

student of a Paris Jewish school; S. May, *Discours prononcé à l'occasion de la distribution des prix de l'Ecole mutuelle israélite de Nancy* (Nancy-Metz, 1841), p. 9; "Souvenirs personnels de Léopold Kahn," *RJL*, 11 (1935), 230.

68. YU, 143; Kahn, *Histoire des écoles*, pp. 106–108.

69. "Un honorable médecin nous a assuré que la mortalité, dans cette école [israélite de Paris], était de 7 p. 100 par an; dans les autres écoles de Paris, proportion gardée, elle n'est que de 2 p. 100." A. [B. B.] Créhange et M. Bolviller, *Lettre au Rédacteur des Archives israélites de France, sur la défense du Consistoire de Paris, par Ben Lévi, dans l'affaire des cimetières de Paris* (Paris, 1841), p. 5.

70. YU, 158, 161, 172; Z. Szajkowski, *Poverty and Social Welfare among French Jews 1800–1880* (New York, 1954), n. 45.

71. *AI*, 4 (1843), 281; Academy of Metz. Department of Moselle. City of Metz. Primary instruction. *Le Comité des écoles municipales israélites de Metz, à ses* coreligionnaires (Metz, 5 March 1846), 2 pp.

72. YU, 74.

73. AN, F17*-141; see Jacques Matter, *De l'éducation des enfants des classes ouvrières et de leur retrait prématuré de l'école* (Strasbourg, 1858).

74. Minutes of meetings at the Nancy school, 30 July 1820 and 20 May 1821 (JTS); *Société d'encouragement au travail en faveur d'Israélites indigents du Bas-Rhin, 1840–1841* (Strasbourg, n.d.), p. 18.

75. See, for example, Consistory of Paris, Committee on Philanthropy. *Compte . . .1858* (Paris, 1859), p. 11.

76. *Ibid.,—1877* (Paris, 1879), pp. 2–10; The Jewish Consistory for the District of Paris . . . *Période de 1866 à 1871* (Paris, n.d.), pp. 22–24; *Rapport sur le functionne-ment de l'Oeuvre des cantines scolaires. Année scolaire 1904–1905* (Paris, 1905); *Rapport présenté au Comité des Dames inspectrices sur le fonctionnement des cantines scolaires* (Paris, 1910), 4 pp.;—(Paris, 1911), 4 pp.; Opening of the school canteens: *Rapport présenté par la Trésorière à la séance du 9 février 1923 sur l'exercice 1921–1922* (Paris, 1923), 13 pp.

77. Lucien de Hirsch, Zadoc Kahn, Gustave de Rothschild, Hospitalières Saint-Gervais, Maternelle de la Place des Vosges. *Comité des Dames inspectrices des écoles et asiles. Rapport sur les Oeuvres complémentaires du Comité des écoles. Exercice 1931–1932* (Paris, 1932), p. 10.

78. Communities, 1836–37.

79. See note 21; *Rapport,* p. 17.

80. YU, Lk 1, p. 25.

81. P. Lévy, "Les écoles juives," p. 540.

82. Minutes of meetings of the Nancy schools (JTS).

83. Szajkowski, *Poverty,* p. 28; YU, 68, 467–75.

84. *Exposé général de la situation de la circonscription consistoriale de Lyon . . . du 1er mars 1863 au 1er mars 1865* (Lyon, 1865), pp. 20, 24.

85. "Prière à l'occasion de la bénédiction des registres des bienfaits et protecteurs des écoles consistoriales de Paris" (see above, note 52; YU, 267); *Extrait du règlement de l'école gratuite d'enseignement mutuel pour la jeunesse israélite de Strasbourg et du département du Bas-Rhin* (Strasbourg, 1820), art. 50.

86. CAHJP, 2.

87. AIU, 421.

88. Szajkowski, "Jewish Vocational Schools," 81–120; *Le Grand rabbin B. Lipman aux fidèles de sa circonscription* (Lille, 1873), p. 12.

89. *Fondation d'une école publique israélite, d'après la méthode d'enseignement mutuel, à Metz* (Metz, 1818), pp. 14–15. See *Le Grand rabbin, par intérim, et le Consistoire israélite de la circonscription de la Moselle, à tous les coreligionnaires du département, et particulièrement aux chefs de famille de la ville de Metz* [Signed: Aron Worms, Jacob-Goudchaux, Béer, Schvabe le Jeune] (Metz, 30 June 1818), 2 pp.

90. YU, 0–1.

91. YU, 437.

92. *Société protectrice de la jeunesse israélite et des arts et métiers de Bayonne. Séance . . . 1867* (Bayonne, 1867), p. 2.

93. T. H. Hallez, *Des Juifs en France* (Paris, 1845), p. 257.

94. Gerson Lévy, *Du paupérisme chez les Juifs. De ses causes et des moyens d'y remédier . . . suivi d'un projet de fondation d'une colonie agricole . . .* (Paris, 1854), p. 35.

95. Maurice Meyer, in *VI, 1* (1860), 153.

96. Ben-Jonas [J. Cohen], in *VI,* 4 (1861), 6–10, 30, 35; Z. Szajkowski, "The Jewish Saint-Simonians. . . ," *Jewish Social Studies,* 9 (1947), 33–60.

97. Extract of the *Archives Israélites* of France. (No. dated September 1846). *Distribution des prix aux écoles israélites de Paris. Discours prononcé à la distribution des prix, aux élèves des Ecoles israélites,* by Mr. Louis Langlois (Paris, 1846), 4 pp.

98. *Distribution des prix faite aux élèves des écoles israélites de Metz, 1823,* p. 14; *1829,* pp. 13–14; see note 22.

99. YU, 529–33.

100. See note 98, *1821,* p. 5; *1824,* p. 9.

101. Edouard de Goldschmidt, *Rapport tendant à introduire l'enseignement de la sténographie dans les écoles consistoriales israélites* (Paris, 5 February 1891), 8 pp.; YU, 515–18, minutes of the Paris school committee, 8 January 1891.

102. Maxime du Camp, *La bienfaisance israélite à Paris* (Paris, 1887), p. 31. Extrait de la *Revue des deux mondes,* 72 (1887), 275–305; *Société des jeunes garçons israélites de Paris.* Extract of the *Archives Israélites* (Paris, May 1850), 4 pp.; *Société des jeunes garçons israélites de Paris* [Review] (Paris, 1858), 15 pp.; Jewish Consistory of Paris. Committee on Philanthropy. *Règlement constitutif de l'orphelinat Salomon de Rothschild, 3 novembre 1857* (Paris, n.d.), 8 pp.; *Orphelinat Salomon et Caroline de Rothschild* (Paris, 1873), 11 pp. (by-laws of 21 October 1873); *Maison de Refuge (Société des Dames israélites) 17, rue Lecouteux à Romainville. Année 1866* (Paris, n.d.), 15 pp.; *Extrait du discours prononcé au Temple de la rue de la Victoire,* by the Chief Rabbi of Paris, 9 December 1876 (Paris, n.d.), 2 pp. ("Maison de Refuge"); *Souscription en faveur de l'hospice des enfants* (Paris, 1864), 3 pp.; *Maison israélite de refuge pour l'enfance, 19, Boulevard de la Saussaye. Neuilly-sur-Seine. Compte rendu. Historique de l'Oeuvre. Edification de la nouvelle maison. Situation financière de l'année 1884* (Paris, 1885), 32 pp.; *Maison israélite de refuge pour l'enfance . . . Compte rendu. Situation financière des années 1885, 1886, 1887* (Paris, 1888), 39 pp.; *Maison de refuge pour l'enfance. . . . Statuts et règlement intérieur* (Paris, 1892), 14 pp.; *Société de refuge du Plessis-Piquet . . . troisième assemblée générale annuelle tenue le 16 juin 1895* (Paris, 1895), 47 pp.; *Exposition universelle de 1900; Refuge du Plessis-Piquet* (Paris, 1900), 51 pp.; *Société du refuge du Plessis-Piquet. Joseph Hirsch, président du Conseil d'administration 1888–1901* (Paris, 1901), 11 pp.; *Oeuvre israélite des colonies scolaires. Statuts* (Paris, 1900), 8 pp. (Paris, 1 March 1900), 3 pp.; *Oeuvre israélite des séjours à la campagne* (previously named the *Oeuvre israélite des Colonies scolaires)* (Paris, 1903), 23 pp.; *Orphelinat israélite de Strasbourg. Compte rendu du Comité administratif. Exercice de 1862* (Strasbourg, 1863), 16 pp.; *Orphelinat*

israelité de Strasbourg (Bas-Rhin). Statuts (Strasbourg, 30 March 1868), 4 pp.; *Jahresbericht des israelitischen Vereins für Feriencolonien* (Strasbourg, 1901-1908); Nathan Netter, *Cent ans d'histoire d'une société de charité messine—La Jeunesse israélite de Metz 1838–1938* (Paris, 1938), 115 pp.

103. Armand Lipman, *Un grand rabbin français. Benjamin Lipman* (Paris, 1923), pp. 419-55. On Jews in prisons, see Jonas Weyl, *Les détenus israélites des maisons centrales* (Strasbourg, 1864), 7 pp.

104. Penel Beaufin, *Législation générale du culte israélite* . . . (Paris, 1894), p. 73.

105. Communities, 3487.

106. Jewish Consistory for the District of Metz, *Reglement relatif aux administrateurs des Temples israélites* . . . (Metz, 1847), art. 2.

107. D. Singer, *Des consistoires,* p. 81; N. Noë, "man of letters" attached to the Public Library of Bordeaux, "Le système d'enseignement primaire israélite est-il en France ce qu'il pourrait être?" *AI,* 4 (1843) 212-19; see also *ibid.,* p. 74; YU, 1452.

108. On similar conflicts in the vocational schools, see Szajkowski, "Jewish Vocational Schools," p. 89.

109. D. Singer, *Des consistoires,* pp. 73-74; S. May, *Discours;* Tsarphati [Olry Terquem], *Neuvième lettre* . . . (Paris, 1837), pp. 30-31; Reform, 534.

110. Committee of Schools, *Estrait du procès-verbal de sa séance du jeudi 14 décembre 1905* (Paris, 1905), 7 pp.

111. See note 22 above.

112. *Relation de l'initiation religieuse de M.E. Nerth, à Sainte-Marie-aux-Mines* (Strasbourg, 1842), pp. 5-6; Jonas Ennery, *Le sentier d'Israël, ou Bible des jeunes israélites* . . . (Paris, 1843, 1861); *The Path of Israel* . . . (London, 1847-50); J. Ennery, *Histoire biblique* . . . (Paris, 1935); *AI,* 10 (1848), 297, 574-78; *UI,* 18 (1863), 527; 35 (1880) 727-28; Paul Muller, "Autour du 24 février dans le Haut-Rhin," *La Révolution de 1848,* 7 (1910), 135; P. Wanwermans, "Les réfugiés du coup d'état en Belgique," *Le Magasin littéraire,* 8-2 (1891), 220; *Dictionnaire des parlementaires français,* (Paris, 1891), II, 575; M. Bloch, *L'Alsace juive depuis la Révolution de 1789* (Guebwiller, 1907), p. 21.

113. Léon Halévy, in *AI,* 1 (1840), 464-67; S. Posener, *Adolphe Crémieux* (Paris, 1933), I, 137; A. Cerfberr, *Biographie alsacienne-lorraine* (Paris, 1879), pp. 85-86; *AI,* 26 (1865), 926, 1052; *UI,* 25 (1869), 62; Jacques Weill, *Méthode pour enseigner l'agriculture* . . . (Paris, 1869); Weill, *Leçons sur la protection et les bons traitements dus aux animaux domestiques* . . . (Paris, 1871); *Notice sur M. D. Lévy-Alvarès* . . . (Versailles, 1861), extract of *Hommes utiles; RI,* 1 (1870), 447; Elie Scheid, *Eugène Manuel* (Paris, 1911), p. 7. About Jews in an educational institution of Lunéville, see Paul Lang, "Les Juifs de Lunéville et la Petite Histoire," *RJL,* 12-129 (1936), 62; Isaac Lévy, *Nathan le Sage.* Conference held by the Vesoul Republican Society of Instruction on 5 December 1880 (Paris, 1881), 51 pp.

114. Alexandre Weill, "Les Juifs de Paris il y a cinquante ans," *La Gerbe* (Paris, 1890), p. 51.

115. *Ibid.*

116. André Spire, *Quelques Juifs et demi-Juifs* (Paris, 1928), I, 206-207.

117. Dr. Hans Kaiser, "Der Kampf gegen die deutsche Sprache in den elsässischen Schulen," *Elsässische Kulturfragen,* 3 (1913), 199, 209, 225; Z. Szajkowski, "The Struggle against Yiddish in France (XVII-XIX centuries), *YIVO-Bleter,* 14 (1939), 69-73; *Statuts* . . . *Colmar* (see note 60 above), p. 9.

118. AN, F17-12514, 12516; M. Chevreuse, *Observations sur les écoles israélites du département de la Moselle,* extract of *Archives Israélites,* 4 (1843), 76-88 (Paris, 1843).

119. Paul Bettelin, *Le Général Marc-François-Jérome Baron Wolff* (n.p., 1942), p. 8; *Notice sur la vie de M. Gerson Lévy* . . . (Metz, 1865), p. v; Z. Szajkowski, "Judaica-Napoleonica. . . ," *Studies in Bibliography and Booklore*, 2 (1956), No. 268.

120. *Fondation d'une école israélite supplémentaire à l'école publique établie d'après la méthode d'enseignement mutuel, à Metz* (Metz, 1819), p. 24; Simon Lévy, *Discours à l'inauguration*, pp. 6, 24; Singer, *Des consistoires*, p. 71.

121. *AI*, 4 (1843), 82; Eugène Manuel, "Souvenirs intimes, un coin du passé," *La Gerbe* (Paris, 1890), p. 45.

122. Paul Lévy, *Histoire linguistique d'Alsace et de Lorraine* (Paris, 1929), II, 112–14, 166, 260; *RI*, 2 (1871), 758.

123. *AI*, 4 (1843), 82.

124. "Société consistoriale pour la propagation des bons livres. Liste de souscription" (Sephardim, 280); L. M. Cottard, *Souvenirs de Moïse Mendelsohn, ou Second livre de lecture des écoles israélites* (Paris-Strasbourg, 1832); J. Hyman, *Premiers éléments de la langue hébraïque* (Paris, 1852); *Précis élémentaire d'instruction religieuse et morale* . . . (Paris, n.d.), 72 pp. As late as 1921 the Alsatian Catholics demanded that religion should be taught in German, *Revue chrétienne*, 69 (1921), 88.

125. "Etre en état de lire un texte hébreu avec la prononciation dite orientale, adopté par tous les grammairiens." Consistoire central des Israélites de France. *A Son Excellence Monsieur le Garde des Sceaux, Ministre de la Justice et des Cultes, le 13 juillet 1847* (Paris, n.d.), p. 7 (Request for aid for a rabbinical school; plan for the by-laws); Singer, *Des consistoires*, p. 76; Tsarphati, in *Journal asiatique*.

126. *AI*, 5 (1844), 459–61.

127. YU, 0–25, 29.

128. *UI*, 63–1 (1907), 134; "A l'occasion des concours qui vont avoir lieu à la fin de mars, M. Reinach exprime une fois encore ses regrets de voir le temps considérable consacré aux études d'hébreu," YU, minutes of meeting, 3 March 1881.

129. *Ibid.*, 4 March 1909.

130. *Zeher Israel* (Paris, n.d.), p. 46.

131. *Association culturelle israélite "Ohel Jacob" de Paris. Statuts* (Paris, 1931).

132. AN, F17-*131, 146–47, 12516; Michel Lévy, *Coup d'oeil historique sur l'état des Israélites en France, et particulièrement en Alsace* (Strasbourg, 1836), p. 19; Kulmann (teacher at Mulhouse), "Histoire de la vie de Ben-Tsaroth, enfant de malheur, ou Mémoires d'un maître d'école israélite de village," *Pure Vérité*, 2 (1847); *AI*, 4 (1843), 285; L. Polack, in *LI*, 4 (1858), 200–204; Emile Lévy, "Un document sur la communauté de Peyrehorade, Landes (1762–1812)," *Annuaire des Archives israélites*, 20 (1903), 48–49.

133. Simon Lévy, *Discours à l'inauguration*, p. 24; "Voilà de quoi encourager nos pauvres qui veulent se livrer à la carrière de l'enseignement," Maurice Meyer, in *VI*, 1 (1860), 158. For a description of a poor Jewish boy who obtained a diploma as a teacher, see Alexandre Weill, *Curonne. Histoire juive* (Paris, 1857), pp. 44–49; Paris Consistory, school cash books; *Note sur le traitement des institutrices des écoles israélites* (Confidential) [Signed:] F. Lévy-Wogue (Paris, March 1912), 4 pp.

134. For a short description of schools of the period, see Eugène Manuel, in *La Gerbe* (Paris, 1890), p. 46; see also note 22.

135. Tama, *Organisation civile*, p. 30; Tourette, *Discours sur les Juifs*, pp. 24–26; *AI*, 4 (1843), 86–87; *UI*, 63–1 (1907), 139; Sephardim, 351.

136. *La Régénération*, 2 (1837), 2; *AI*, 4 (1843), 126.

137. Daniel Stauben, *Scènes de la vie juive en Alsace* (Paris, 1860), pp. 79–80; M. Gins-

burger, "Duttlenheim," *Souvenir et Science,* 3-3 (1932), 10; D. Schornstein, "Perle. . .," *RI,* 3 (1872), 797-99, 811-13; 4 (1873), 76-80.

138. *Dictionnaire de biographie française* (Paris, 1954), VI, 682; Jules Bauer, *L'Ecole rabbinique de France* (Paris, 1930), pp. 183-84.

139. "Le professeur soit israélite ou chrétien aura son logement dans le local de l'école," YU, 24; Sephardim, 1059-62; Daily reports of the 1840s signed by August Fenouil (Communities, pp. 3225-73); YU, minutes, 14 April 1887.

140. *Liste des membres composant la Société populaire de Strasbourg . . . 25 vendémiaire, l'an trois* (n.p., n.d.); CAHJP, 1.

141. *La Régénération,* 2 (1837), 4; ". . .les ouvrages d'Histoire sainte . . . et qui sont signés: Villemeureux, revu par l'abbé Fauvel ou l'abbé Drioux," Séligmann Lévy, in *RI,* 1 (1870), 248.

142. Kulmann, *Histoire de Ben-Tsaroth,* pp. 540-41; Michel-A. Weill, "Le Grand rabbin Salomon Ulmann, souvenirs de jeunesse," *UI,* 20 (1865), 527-28.

143. Until World War II over 150 Jewish textbooks and histories were published.

144. *A1 B1* (Sélestat, n.d.), alphabet hébreu-allemand; N. Noé, [14] *Tableaux pour apprendre à lire l'hébreu . . .* (Bordeaux, 1820); Noé, *Tableau synoptique . . .* (n.p., n.d.); Lacour, *Rapport sur l'application fait par M. Noé, de la méthode de l'enseignement. . . de la langue hébraïque* (Bordeaux, 1820).

145. *Distribution des prix . . . Metz, 1827,* p. 15; F. Sarchi, *Grammaire hébraïque . . .* (Paris, 1828).

146. P. Beaufin, *Législation générale,* p. 73; *Réflexions générales sur un projet d'ordonnance relatif à une nouvelle organisation du culte israélite* (Metz, 1839), p. 2.

147. "Société israélite des livres moraux et religieux," *AI,* 13 (1852), 618-20; "Société des bons livres de Strasbourg," *ibid.,* p. 668; *Société des livres moraux et religieux* (Poissy, 1852); 3 pp.; Benjamin Gradis, *De la Société israélite des livres moraux et religieux* (Paris, 1854); *Société consistoriale pour la propagation des bons livres* (Strasbourg, n.d.), 2 pp.; *AI,* 14 (1853), 21-22, 221-23; 15 (1854), 98-103, 171-72.

148. Alexandre Ben-Baruch Créhange, *Des Droits et des devoirs du citoyen . . .* (Paris, 1848); Elie Lambert, *Les Saintes semences . . .* (Metz, 1853); *Précis élémentaire d'instruction religieuse . . .* (Paris, n.d.); Betting de Lancastel, *Considérations,* pp. 68-69; Salomon Ulmann, *Recueil d'instructions . . .* (Strasbourg, 1843).

149. Paul Klein, "Mauvais juif, mauvais chrétien," *Revue de la pensée juive,* 7 (1951), 89.

150. Léon Halévy, *Résumé de l'histoire des juifs modernes* (Paris, 1828); L. M. Lambert, *Précis de l'histoire des Hébreux, depuis le Patriarche Abraham jusqu'en 1840* (Metz, 1840); J. Bédarride, *Les Juifs en France, en Italie et en Espagne* (Paris, 1859); Moïse Schwab, *Histoire des Israélites . . .* (Paris, 1866); Elie Aristide Astruc, *Histoire abrégée des Juifs . . .* (Paris, 1869); *RI,* 1 (1870), 24-27, 72, 74, 88-92, 101-104, 110-11, 128-38, 145-48, 152-54, 177-78, 198-200, 206, 273-76, 305-307.

151. YU, minutes of meetings, 1 January 1876; 9 November 1883; 7 February, 30 April and 15 July 1885; Lacour, *Rapport par Noé.*

152. YU, minutes of meeting, 4 March 1909.

153. CAHJP, 17. See also Elie Aristide Astruc, *Enseignement normal de l'histoire des Hébreux* (Paris, 1881), extract from the *Revue pédagogique.*

154. S. Dubnow, *Précis d'histoire juive . . .* (Paris, 1936); David Fresco, *Histoire des Israélites. . .* (Paris, 1898); Fresco, *Histoire des peuples modernes . . .* (n.p., n.d.).

155. [Jirmijja ben Meinster Heinemann] *Religions-Bekenntnis für Israeliten . . .* (Vienna, 1813).

156. Consistoire israélite de Vesoul . . . *A Messieurs les membres des commissions adminis-tratives des communautés israélites* . . . [Signed:] Moïse Schuhl, chief rabbi (Vesoul, 7 April 1895), 3 pp. ("Il faudrait fonder dans chaque communauté une Bibliothèque israélite"); *L'Echo sioniste*, 1-10 (1899), 145-46.

157. Eugénie-Rebecca Rodrigues Foa (Gradis), *Les Saintes . . . Sainte Geneviève . . .* (Paris, 1841), 61 pp.; and her, *La Madone, suivi du Tuteur* (Paris, Les Petits livres de M. le Curé, 1845), 64 pp.

158. Drach, *De l'harmonie*, I, 37; YU, 492; Central Consistory of the Jews of France. *A MM. les Membres des Consistoires départementaux, et à MM. les Notables des circonscriptions respectives* (Paris, 22 November 1822), 4 pp.; S. Ulmann, *Lettre pastorale adressée par le Grand rabbin du Consistoire central à MM. les Grands rabbins, rabbins communaux et à tous ses coreligionnaires de France* (Paris, 23 October 1860), p. 4; *SIW*, 12 August 1908, p. 19; see also: *Extrait du registre des délibérations du Consistoire israélite de la circonscription de Metz. Séance du 15 novembre 1820* (Metz, 1820), 8 pp. (By-laws for a school of Talmud); Tsarphati [Olry Terquem], *Sixième lettre . . . sur l'établissement d'une école de théologie à Paris, et sur la suppression des écoles talmudiques en province . . .* (Paris, 1824); Ministère de l'Intérieur, *Arrêté qui autorise l'établissement d'une Ecole rabbi-nique à Metz* [21 August 1829, with by-laws for the Central Rabbinical School of Metz] (Paris, n.d.), 16 pp.; *Règlement général d'administration pour le Séminaire israélite établi à Paris par décret impérial du 1er juillet 1859* (Paris, 1 December 1860), 22 pp.; *Rapport sur la situation morale du Séminaire israélite, suivi de la Vie de Hillel l'Ancien . . . Par Isaac Trénel . . . L'Esclavage selon la Bible et le Talmud . . . Par Zadoc Kahn* (Paris, 1867), 203 pp.

159. M. Weiskopf and Zadoc Kahn, *Discours prononcés à l'inauguration du nouvel oratoire de la Société de l'Etude talmudique . . . 12 septembre 1884* (Paris, 1884), 31 pp.; Kahn, *Histoire des écoles*, p. 70; Isidore Loeb, *Biographie d'Albert Cohn* (Paris, 1878), p. 40; "Le nombre de plus en plus insuffisant de jeunes gens se destinant au Rabbinat. Si le Talmud-Thora n'existait pas, le recrutement des ministres de notre culte deviendrait tout à fait impossible, car il est presque sans exemple qu'un jeune homme reçoive ailleurs la préparation nécessaire . . ." *Le Grand rabbin du Consistoire central des Israélites de France* [Signed:] Zadoc Kahn (Paris, 25 January 1901), 2 pp.; *Extrait des Archives israélites de France* (July and August, 1840). *Rapport lu dans la séance du 28 avril 1840, par M. [Adolphe] Crémieux* (Paris, 1840), p. 19; *La Paix*, 1847, 361-65; *Société talmudique. Statuts* (Paris, n.d.), 1 p.; Benjamin Gradis, *De la nouvelle école talmudique fondée à Paris* (Bordeaux, 17 May 1853). On an Alsatian rabbi and his students, see Jos. Bloch, "Ernest Weill," *RJL*, 8 February 1856. On the Alsatian rabbinical school after the German annexation of the province, see *Rabbinervorbildungs-Schule von Elsass-Lothringen . . . École préparatoire rabbinique d'Alsace-Lorraine. Rapport . . .* (Colmar, 1885); *Rabbiner-Seminar Colmar. Séminaire rabbinique de Colmar. Bericht . . . seit seiner Gründung (1880–81) bis Juli 1893* (Colmar, 1893).

160. *Israelitisches Elsass-Lothringen. L'Alsace-Lorraine israélite* (Mulhouse), 2 (1878), 13.

161. S. Posener, *Adolph Crémieux*, p. 489; *AI*, 4 (1843) 345-47; Martin, *Mémoire présenté au Conseil supérieur de l'instruction publique pour M. Jérôme Aron . . .* (Paris, 1850), 15 pp.; Chamber of Deputies, *Opinion de M. Voyer d'Argenson, Député du departement du Haut-Rhin, sur la pétition des Protestants de Bordeaux* (Paris, n.d.), 20 pp.; *UI*, 5 (1849), 119, 127, 300; 7 (1851), 97; *AI*, 13 (1852), 430-31; "Extrait des délibérations . . . ," *RJL*, 9-94, 99; *Le Progrès de l'Est*, 12 July 1881.

162. Eugène Manuel, *Lettres de jeunesse* (Paris, 1900), p. 58; Maurice Mayer, in *AI*, 5 (1844), 246-54; Alexandre Weill, "Juifs de Paris," *La Gerbe* (Paris, 1890), p. 51; "A l'époque ou votre père [Samuel Cahen] était encore un jeune homme, les carrières libérales étaient

presque toutes fermées aux Juifs"; Z. Szajkowski, "The Struggle for Jewish Emancipation in Algeria after the French Occupation," *Historia Judaica* (1956), 31.

163. YU, 1445; E. A. Astruc, *Oraison funèbre du vénérable David Marx* . . . (Paris, 1864); "Extrait des délibérations . . . ," *RJL*, 9-91-92, 94.

164. *AI*, 5 (1844), 667; *Institution Springer*. 34-36, rue de la Tour d'Auvergne. Paris. *Année scolaire 1884–1885. Palmarès* (Paris, 1885) 24 pp.; —*Année scolaire 1892–1893. Palmarès* (Paris, 1893), 39 pp.

165. Michel Berr, *Observations*, p. 14; Z. Szajkowski, "Michel Berr," *The Journal of Jewish Studies*, 14 (1963), 58.

166. "Les garçons suivaient intelligemment leurs études au lycée . . . les filles . . . portaient déjà coquettement la toilette," Henry Léon, "Etude de moeurs juives . . . ," *Bulletin de la Société des sciences et arts de Bayonne* (1900), 157; Léon, *Histoire de Bayonne*, pp. 366-68; *AI*, 15 (1854), 226-27; 19 (1858), 334-36.

167. YU, minutes of meetings, 7 May 1874 and 1 April 1875; R.T., in *UI*, 51 (1897), 581-84; Salomon Lubetzki, *ibid.*, pp. 685-88. See also Appendix II.

168. Lycées Janson de Sailly, Lakanal, Michelet, Montaigne, Louis-le-Grand, Saint-Louis; YIVO questionnaire about Paris' Jewish organizations in 1939 (Tcherikower).

169. *L'Echo sioniste*, 1-8 (1899), 122.

170. *AI*, 5 (1844), 459-60; Sephardim, 1052 (1843): "L'importance du but de ce cours, n'a pas besoin, Messieurs, d'être démontrée: elle se fait assez sentir, par le vide qu'a laissé à Bordeaux l'absence du Talmud Torah, renversé avec beaucoup d'institutions utiles. Par l'ignorance trop générale de la langue hébraïque qui nous prive de hazanim instruits et de professeurs habiles; et lorsque les restes des anciennes générations auront disparu de notre kehila, cette pénurie d'hommes versés dans les saintes écritures se fera ressentir davantage. Mais une raison plus puissante encore et que vous avez dû apprécier depuis longtemps, c'est que le désordre qui règne au Temple, est principalement entretenu par l'ignorance de la langue dans laquelle sont écrites nos prières"; René Hirschler, *Juifs à Mulhouse*, p. 14; *Consistoire israélite de la circonscription de Paris* (Paris, 31 October 1841), 1 p.: "Des cours gratuits d'instruction religieuse et morale . . . dont MM. S. Munk et A. Cohn ont spontanément offert de se charger"; Jewish Consistory for the District of Paris. Community Fund. School Committee. *Culte et instruction* (Paris, n.d.), poster: "Des cours réguliers de la langue hébraïque seraient ouverts à l'usage des adultes" [Signed:] Albert Cohn, S. H. Goldschmidt, S. Hauser, G. Fribourg, J. Hayem, E. Hendlé; *ibid.* (Paris, 14 January 1876), 2 pp.; (1 January 1877), 2 pp. See *Société scientifique littéraire israélite* (Paris, 1865), 3 pp.; *Cours littéraire*, report by Hippolyte Rodrigues, permanent secretary of the Société scientifique littéraire israélite (Paris, 1866), 14 pp.; Benjamin Mossé, in *LI*, 1 (1858), 166; *Appel aux pères de familles israélites de France et de l'étranger* [Signed:] Dietz (Avignon, 1848); "Association bayonnaise d'études juives," Sephardim, 746.

171. YU, 430-31. On students of the Metz rabbinical school who were also private teachers, see Justin Dennery, "La Communauté israélite de Metz avant 1870," *UI* (1925), 291. See A. A. Seybot, *Das alte Strassburg* (Strasbourg, 1890), p. 173; Drach, *De l'harmonie*, I, 40, 44, 47; CAHJP, 16-17; Rabbi Jacques Lévi of Valenciennes in 1871 had a private dormitory for students of the city's lycée and also took care of their religious education for the price of one thousand francs per student. *LI*, 1 (1855), 89; *RI*, 2 (1871), 832.

172. Kahn, *Histoire des écoles*, p. 66; E. Manuel, "Souvenirs intimes," p. 45; A. B.-B. Créhange, *Annuaire* . . . *5619* (Paris, 1858), announcement; *FJ*, 4 (1862-63), 21-27; *Distribution des prix* . . . *Metz 1826*, p. 17, *1832*, p. 13; "Extrait. . . ," *RJL*, 4-35 (1928), 84; *FJ*, 4 (1862-63), 21-27; YU, 458-65.

173. Léon, *Histoire de Bayonne,* pp. 365–66; YU, 53–54. See also *Pensionnat dirigé par M. Isaac Mayer, instituteur à Francfort-sur-le-Mein, No. 4, Hinter der schoenen Aussicht* (n.p., ca. 1852); *Sussex House à Douvres (Folkestone House)* (n.p., ca. 1853); *AI,* 26 (1865), 317 ("Institut commercial et industriel à Bruxelles"); YU, 034–35; *Fondation d'un établissement d'instruction secondaire israélite á Saint-Esprit (Landes)* [Signed:] L. Marx, chief rabbi (n.p., 22 February 1854), 2 pp.; *Une institution secondaire israélite vient de s'ouvrir à Bayonne* [Signed:] Les professeurs Rheims et Lion (Bayonne, 1850); *Rheims et Lion, les professeurs* (Bayonne, 1860), 1 p. (Opening of a Jewish secondary school); *Isaac Alvarès Deléon, professeur de langues* (Bordeaux, 25 October 1824), 1 p.; *Circulaire* [Signed:] Jacob de Soria, Isaac Alvarès Deléon (Bordeaux, 21 April 1828), 1 p. ("Projetant d'établir une école pour l'instruction des jeunes israélites de Bordeaux"); *Prospectus* (Bordeaux, 1842), 3 pp. (Educational institution directed by Dames Fonséca and Lange); *Maison d'éducation pour les jeunes gens dirigée par M. Lion. Prospectus* (Bordeaux, n.d.), 2 pp.; *Pensionnats israélites de Lyon pour jeunes gens et demoiselles* [Signed:] Rabbi Weinberg (Lyon, 1855), 1 p.; *Institution israelite de jeunes gens, dirigée par M. A. Franck, licencié ès sciences, secrétaire du Consistoire israélite, à Lyon, place des Celéstins, 5* (n.p., 1860), 1 p.; *Pensionnat de garçons. Rue de l'Arsenal, no. 39 à Metz* (Metz, 1851), 1 p.; *Pensionnat de garçons de M. J. Bloch, rue de l'Arsenal, à Metz* (Metz, 1857), 1 p.; *Pensionnat de demoiselles de Mme J. Kahn. 22, rue Boileau, Auteuil—Paris* (Paris, 1870), 2 pp.; *Mademoiselle N. Blum a l'honneur d'informer les familles israélites des Batignoles . . .* (n.p., 1870), 1 p. ("qu'elle ouvrira un cours gratuit d'enseignement religieux et de préparation à l'initiation . . . "); *Rue Cadet 10. Externat de 20 élèves, avec un grand jardin;* directed by M. Cahun, former director of the Jewish school in Haguenau (Paris, n.d.), 2 pp.; *Institution française-allemande dirigée par M. Hermann . . .* (Paris, 1851), 1 p.; *Education universitaire.* Institution Jauffret. 6, Place Royale, à Paris. (n.p., 1863), 1 p.; *Maison d'éducation des jeunes gens dirigée par M. Kahn, 14 rue Portefoin, à* Paris (n.p., 1852), 1 p.; *Maison d'éducation de Mme Marix à Auteuil, rue Boileau 52 et 54. Ci-devant à Paris, No. 4, rue du grand Chantier* (n.p., 1854), 1 p.; *Institution rue Turgot 11* directed by M. Jules Rosenfeld (Paris, 1860), 1 p.; *Jules Rosenfeld, Institution de jeunes gens. Discours prononcé à la distribution des prix, le 14 août 1860,* by the director (Paris, 1860), 8 pp.; *Discours prononcé à la distribution des prix le 7 août 1863* (Paris, 1863), 15 pp.; *Cabinet du Grand rabbin du Consistoire central de France* [Signed:] Isidor (Paris, 4 June 1867), 1 p. ("Monsieur et Madame Schneider, appelés et appuyés par le Comité consistorial de Paris, viennent de fonder sous notre inspriation une école israélite"); *Institution de jeunes israélites dirigée par M. [Joseph] et Mme [Céline] Schneider. 96,* Boulevard de la Tour-Maubourg (Paris, 1 July 1867), 2 pp.

174. Maurice Meyer, in *VI,* 1 (1860), 152; Isidore Cahen, student at l'Ecole Normale, *Deux libertés en une* (Paris, 1848), 71 pp.

175. *AI,* 9 (1848), 207.

176. I. Uhry, *Recueil des lois . . .* (Bordeaux, 1878), II, 125.

177. Leaflets of the Society, 25 October 1881 and 1 December 1883; *L'Union scolaire. Association amicale des anciens élèves israélites des écoles consistoriales et communales de Paris. Règlement, Juillet 1882* (Vincennes, 1882), 15 pp.; *Union scolaire. Bulletin mensuel* (Paris), No. 1, November 1906; No. 187, 15 April 1933.

178. Ministery of Public Instruction and Culture. Administration of Culture; Division of non-Catholics. *Avis de principe émis par le Conseil d'Etat en 1873, touchant les libéralités faites aux établissements ecclésiastiques* (Paris, October 1873), 42 pp.; *Messieurs et chers coreligionnaires* (Paris, 25 October 1881), 6 pp.: "Il devient nécessaire de prendre toute une série de mesures propres à rendre à l'instruction religieuse la place qu'elle a perdue."

Pp. 3-6: "Rapport . . . du 12 octobre 1881 . . . Considérant que l'instruction religieuse a cessé de faire partie des matières exigées pour le brevet élémentaire. . . "; Jewish Consistory of Paris. Community Fund. *Culte et instruction* (Paris, December 1885), 3 pp.: "La loi de 1882, qui a exclu l'enseignement religieux du programme des écoles primaires, nous a mis dans la nécessité d'instituer des cours de religion pour les quinze cents enfants"; Rabbi Moïse Metzger, *L'Instruction religieuse et la laïcisation des écoles.* Sermon delivered at the Synagogue de Belfort on Yom Kippur 5648 (28 September 1887) (Paris, 1889), 24 pp.; *Observations de la Cour des Comptes. Rapport au Président de la République,* page 71 (—78). *Inapplication aux Consistoires israélites de la Loi du 26 janvier 1842* (n.p., n.d.), 11 pp.; Conseil d'Etat. Section of the Interior. *Mémoire pour le Consistoire israélite de Paris.* [Signed:] Léonce Lehmann (Paris, n.d.), pp. 3-4: ". . . sur l'acceptation de divers legs faits au Consistoire israélite de Paris pour des oeuvres d'instruction ou de charité"; *Décret du 27 mars portant règlement d'administration des Consistoires israélites* (Paris, 1893), 16 pp.; Armand Lods, *Etude critique du décret sur la comptabilité des conseils presbytéraux . . .* (Paris, 1893), 59 pp.; Albert Manuel, "Les Consistoires israélites de France. . . . " *REJ,* 83 (1926), 525-27; *The Jewish Chronicle,* 8 June 1906, p. 14; *UI,* 60-2 (1905), 37-40, 75-80, 133-37 ("De la prohibition des dons et legs en faveur des associations religieuses").

179. Szajkowski, "The Influence of the Separation of the Church from the State on the Franco-Jewish Communities," *Davke* (Buenos Aires), 21 (1954), 382-92.

180. Emile Lévy, *La morale religieuse et la morale laïque.* Response to the Congress of Free Thought. Two sermons . . . (Bayonne, 1905), 23 pp.; see also *AI,* 68 (1907), 713; 69 (1908), 201-203.

181. *Rapport présenté à Messieurs les membres du Consistoire de Paris,* by Mr. Engelman (Paris, n.d.), 15 pp.: "La situation faite aux écoles primaires israélites depuis que les pouvoirs publics ont contesté aux Consistoires le droit de s'en occuper"; *Association pour le développement de l'instruction élémentaire et professionnelle* (Paris, ca. 1906), 5 pp.; Rabbi Mayer Lambert, *Rapport sommaire sur les réformes à introduire dans l'enseignement religieux* (Belfort, 14 May 1907), 1 + 7 pp.; Rabbi Moïse Metzger, *Union du Rabbinat français. Culte public et instruction religieuse* (Belfort, 14 May 1907), 7 pp.; The French section of the International Workers. 4th section, *Les écoles juives de la ville de Paris* (Paris, 1907), 6 pp.; YU, 522, 578-83, 596-597, 796; YU, 521. See *UI,* 62-1 (1907), 709-14, 63-2 (1908), 364-70; see *Jewish Chronicle,* 3 May 1907. On the Jewish schools of Paris after the separation, see also *Bulletin de l'Association amicale des anciens élèves des écoles Halphen et Lucien de Hirsch* (Paris, 1908), I. *Bulletin de l'Association amicale des anciens élèves des écoles communales de la rue des Tournelles et de la rue des Hospitalières Saint-Gervais* (Paris, January 1932), No. 28.

182. Edmund Silberner, "Austrian Social Democracy and the Jewish Problem," *Historia Judaica,* 13 (1951), 139-40.

183. Scheid, *Eugène Manuel,* p. 11.

184. "Alliance de la jeunesse israélite et d'encouragement aux arts et métiers," Communities, 2626-32.

185. Bayonne (3), Belfort (2), Besançon (2), Bordeaux (3), Lyon (2), Marseilles (3), Nîmes (2), Paris (3). "Rapport sur la situation religieuse, morale et administrative des Israélites de France et d'Algérie," p. 39 (JTS); Aix, Avignon, Boulogne, Carpentras, Châlons-sur-Marne, Clermont, Dijon, Dunkerque, Epernay, Lille, Nancy, Nantes, Nice, Orange, Reims, Saint-Etienne, Saint-Quentin, Sedan, Toul, Toulouse, Valenciennes, Vesoul, Vitry (*ibid.*).

186. *Keren ha-sefer ve-hahinukh* (Paris, 1947), p. 2.

187. See also YU, minutes of meetings, 9 and 28 October 1902.

188. On prayers in schools, see *RI*, 2 (1870), 786; *Chers coreligionnaires* [Signed:] Zadoc Kahn (Paris, 5 October 1871), 1 p.: ". . . la nécessité qu'il y a de donner à la jeunesse israélite une instruction religieuse forte et sérieuse"; *Chers coreligionnaires* [Signed:] Zadoc Kahn (Paris, November 1872), 1 p.: "Le service religieux du Samedi, institué spécialement pour les enfants"; Z. S. [Szajkowski], "Jewish Communal Life in Paris," *Jews in France* (New York, 1942), II, 242, in Yiddish; YIVO questionnaire of the Paris Jewish organization, 1939 (Tcherikower).

189. *UI*, 1863, 14; *Annuaire israélite pour l'année du monde 5593* . . . (Paris, 1832: "Réflexions sur la manière de célébrer la majorité religieuse"; *Initiation religieuse de jeunes filles israélites*, celebrated in the consistorial Temple of Marseilles, 28 March 1842. [Signed:] Hauser aîné (Marseilles, n.d.), 4 pp.; Albert Cohn, *Examen d'un israélite à l'âge de treize ans* (Paris, 1842), xiii + 95 pp.; Armand Aron, *Le Grand rabbin du Consistoire israélite de la circonscription de Strasbourg à MM. les rabbins et commissaires-surveillants près des synagogues* (Strasbourg, 9 March 1843); *Programme et discours à l'occasion de l'initiation religieuse de neuf jeunes filles israélites de Sarrebourg*, celebrated on 27 August 1842 . . . in the synagogue of this city, by M. L. Isidor . . . (Strasbourg, 1843); L. Klotz, rabbi of Lunéville, *Sermon prononcé à la cérémonie de l'initiation religieuse célébrée dans le Temple israélite de Blâmont, le 5 septembre 1846* . . . (Saint-Nicolas-de-Port, n.d.), 16 pp.; A. Ben-Baruch Créhange, *Offrande pure . . . suivi du programme de la cérémonie de l'initiation* (n.p., n.d.); (Extract from *Archives Israélites.*) *Initiation religieuse à Marseille* (Paris, August 1850); Lion Mayer Lambert, *Initiation religieuse* (Metz, 1852), 6 pp.; *Programme de l'initiation religieuse des filles israélites, adopté par le Consistoire israélite de Marseille* (Marseilles, 1852); Jacques Weinberg, *Sermons prononcés dans le Temple israélite de Lyon . . . 5615* (Lyon, 1855), pp. 25–31: "Sermon prononcé le jour de Simhat Thora 5615 à l'occasion de l'initiation religieuse des enfants des deux sexes"; *Prière pour l'enfance après l'initiation religieuse* (n.p., 1861), 1 p.; *Discours prononcé au Temple israélite de Metz par le rabbin Eliézer Lambert à l'occasion de la cérémonie religieuse des jeunes filles, célébrée le deuxième jour de Schabouoth* (Metz, 1862); *Initiation religieuse des jeunes filles, fixée au deuxième jour de Schabouoth 5622, à deux heures de l'après-midi.* Program (Metz, n.d.), 2 pp.; *Le Grand rabbin de Metz aux Israélites de sa circonscription.* [Signed:] Benjamin Lipman (Metz, 28 March 1866), 3 pp.; Isaac Uhry, *Sepher Moreh. Guide pour l'initiation religieuse des jeunes israélites des deux sexes, du rite portugais* (Bordeaux, 1870); Consistory of Paris. *Règlement concernant la célébration de la Bar-Mitzwa.* [Signed:] Zadoc Kahn (Paris, 25 September 1873), 1 p.; *Services de Min'ha les samedis avec prédications et initiation* [Signed:] Zadoc Kahn (Paris, 2 November 1876), 3 pp.; *Programme de la cérémonie de l'initiation religieuse à Paris* (Paris, 1874), 2 pp.; 1877, 8 pp.; 1880, 14 pp.; *Le Grand rabbin de Paris* [Signed:] Z. Kahn (Paris, 4 January 1883), 2 pp.; *Cérémonie de l'initiation religieuse* (Marseilles, n.d.); Moïse Israël Binding [*Bar Mitsvah Sermon*] (Metz, 1816), in Hebrew; *Discours de S. de Cologna, prononcé le 11 août 1838, à Paris, dans le Temple israélite, par Adolphe Crémieux, à l'occasion de sa majorité religieuse* (Paris, n.d.), 7 pp.; B. Zeitlin, *Parole de l'Alliance ou Instruction religieuse à l'usage de la jeunesse israélite. Composé pour l'initiation religieuse du jeune Myrtile Mayer, célébrée à Metz, le 5 mars 1847* (Metz, 1847); Léon Hollaenderski, *Bar-Mitzwa. 13e anniversaire d'Edmond, baron de Rothschild, célébré . . . le 2 octobre 1858* (Paris, 1858), 13 pp.; *Discours prononcés au Temple consistorial israélite de Paris le samedi de Hanouca, l'an 5619 (14 décembre 1858) à l'occasion de l'inauguration d'un Sepher Thora donné par M.*

Albert Cohn le jour où son fils, Samson Cohn, a célebre sa majorité religieuse. Suivis du discours prononcé le même jour par le jeune Samson Cohn (Paris, 1858), 22 pp.; Vittorio Giavi, *Allocution prononcée dans le Temple israélite réformé [de Nice] 1e 24 janvier 1874, à l'occasion de l'initiation religieuse de Léon Schwartz* (Paris, 1874), 6 pp.; Giavi, *Allocution prononcée dans le Temple israélite réformé de Nice, à l'occasion de l'initiation religieuse des élèves S. R. Dalsème et E. Schwartz* (Nice, 1875), 12 pp.; "The Jews of France—Their present and Future," *The American Hebrew,* 24 January 1908, p. 305.

190. Szajkowski, *Poverty,* p. 75. On the life of immigrant pupils, see L. Dori [Isidore Loeb], "Joseph Iselwicz," *RI,* 1 (1870), 187. Course of religious instruction at rue Nicolet; kindergarten, place des Vosges; Talmud Torah; kindergarten, rue des Hospitalières, YU, 366–80.

191. YU, minutes of meetings, 26 October 1882; 28 August 1903; 19 April 1904; 9 May 1906.

192. YU, 1100, 1118, 1150, 1237.

193. *UI,* 63-2 (1908), 72; YU; minutes of meetings, 12 June 1918: "Nous avons dû classer . . . distinguer les Français et les étrangers si nombreux dans nos écoles—et parmi ces derniers, ceux qui avaient servi dans nos armées ou dans les armées alliées ou ceux qui ne l'avaient même pas essayé"; Z. Szajkowski, *Analytical Franco-Jewish Gazetteer 1939–1945* (New York, 1966), p. 23.

194. Szajkowski, "Jewish Communal Life in Paris," pp. 238–41; M. Feldman, "Supplementary schools of the Kultur-Liga," *10 ior kultur lige. Zamlbukh* (Paris, 1932), 46–47; *Unzer kind,* published by the "Fraynd fun arbeter kind," 1 (May 1936), *Nayer dor,* published by Colonie Scolaire, 1 (15 August 1930).

195. *Shpeizers kalendar* (Paris, 1911), p. 55.

196. Association cultuelle orientale," Sephardim, 1855-56. *La Protection de l'enfance séfaradite. Statuts* (Paris, 1931), 4 pp.; YIVO questionnaire of 1939 (Tcherikower).

197. YU, 458–65; Dr. H. Engelbert, *Statistik des Judenthums im deutschen Reich. . .* (Frankfurt am Mein, 1875), pp. 85–90.

198. Betting de Lancastel, *Considérations,* p. 68; Th. Hallez, *Juifs en France,* p. 257; Grimaud, *Histoire de la liberté,* vi, 146; *RI,* 2 (1871), 764.

199. YU, 467–75; *LI,* September 1857, 141, 144–45; Engelbert, *Statistik des Judenthums,* pp. 85–90.

200. Justin Dennery, "Communauté de Metz," p.298; YU, 430–31; AN, F17-131 (Moselle), 140 (Bas-Rhin), 141 (Haut-Rhin); Engelbert, *Statistik des Judenthums,* pp. 85–90; Arthur Weill, "L'école primaire israélite en Alsace et en Lorraine (1870-1923)," *UI,* 68 (1923), 109–10; Ad. Worms, *Rapport fait au nom du Comité cantonal* [des écoles] (Metz, 1827), 10 pp.; Gerson-Lévy, *Rapport fait au nom du Comité d'administration des écoles israélites* (Metz, 1819), 12 pp.;—1820, 16 pp.

201. Arthur Weill, "L'école primaire," pp. 109–10.

202. Alexis Alexandre, David Azévédo, Jacob Pereyra Soarez, Abraham Oxéda (business theory course), Joseph Andrade (son of the chief rabbi), Abraham Oxéda (Imperial School of Navigation), Henri Worms, Jacob Dias, Isaac Dias (School of Design), J[osep]h Emile Lopes Pereyra, G[abri]el Félix Lopes Pereyra (Lycée), YU, 1-5; YU, 22, 46, 55–80; Simon Lévy, *Discours à l'inauguration,* p. 3; *Journal d'éducation,* 12 (1840), 295; 13 (1841), 87; A. Denis, *Histoire de l'enseignement public à Bordeaux 1414–1910* (Bordeaux, 1913), p. 164; Th. Malvezin, *Histoire des Juifs à Bordeaux* (Bordeaux, 1875), p. 323; E. Féret, *Statistique générale. . . de la Gironde,* 1 (Bordeaux, 1878), 320, 365.

203. YU, 1-5.

204. *Société protectrice de la jeunesse israélite et des arts et métiers de Bayonne. Séance publique du 15 octobre 1900*, p. 21 ("Je ne regrette pas cette transformation car j'estime que l'instruction profane gagne à être donnée séparément"); Jewish Cultural Association of Bayonne, *Exercice 1930. Assemblée générale* (Bayonne, 1931), p. 2; —*1936*, p. 4; Léon, *Histoire de Bayonne*, pp. 247-48, 290-91, 371; YU, 44.

205. Circular, Marseilles, 12 August 1818 [Signed:] J. Altaras, G. V. Cavaglieri (Marseilles, 1818), 3 pp.; YU, 126; *Compte-rendu de la gestion du Consistoire israélite de Marseille pendant les années 1863, 1864 et 1865* (Marseilles, 1866), pp. 29-30; —*années 1877, 1878, 1879, 1880 et 1881* (Marseilles, 1882), pp. 15-16; *Les Bouches-du-Rhône. Encyclopédie départementale* (Paris-Marseilles, 1923), p. 702.

206. "Règlement de la Société des Dames protectrices des pauvres enfants israélites d'Avignon," YU, 1430-31; Benjamin Mossé, *Progrès social et religieux dans les communautés israélites du département du Vaucluse* (Avignon, 1861), p. 1; Jonas Weyl, *Consistoire israélite de Marseille. Séance du dimanche 12 avril 1885. Etat religieux des communautés de l'ancien Comtat Arba Kehilith, Vaucluse, Gard, Hérault, Bouches-du-Rhône (moins Marseille)*. . . (Marseilles, 1885), p. 7. See M. D. Cohen, *Le Grand rabbin du Consistoire israélite à ses coreligionnaires de Marseille et de la circonscription* (Marseilles, 21 March 1852), 4 pp.: "Nîmes et Lyon possèdent, à notre instar, des écoles gratuites destinées à l'instruction de la jeunesse infortunée. Carpentras même s'est éveillée de sa longue léthargie et vient d'ouvrir un pareil établissement"; Alfred Lévy, *Notice sur les Israélites de Lyon* (Paris, 1894), p. 39. On other Jewish schools, see *AI*, 2 (1841), 542-43 (a school with 30 students existed since 1837 in Bourbonne-les-Bains and was subventioned by the city); *Communauté israélite de la circonscription de Lille. Establissement d'une école* [Signed:] C. B. Scriber l'aîné, Kauffmann, Oury Cahen, Léonard Bloch (Lille, 20 April 1843), 1 p.; Isaac Lévy, rabbi in Verdun, *Discours prononcé à la distribution des prix du cours d'instruction religieuse à Verdun, le dernier jour de Pâques 5622, 22 avril 1862* (n.p., n.d.), 4 pp.; Isidor Loeb, [Circular to the Jewish community of Saint-Etienne about religious instruction] (Saint-Etienne, 1868), 8 pp.; Moïse Netter, rabbi of Saint-Etienne, *L'Instruction religieuse et l'avenir du judaïsme*. Sermon delivered during Passover 5650 [6 April 1890] (Paris, 1890), 16 pp.; J. Weinberg, *Lettre de M. le Grand rabbin de Lyon à ses coreligionnaires de cette ville* (Lyon, 2 January 1873), 4 pp.; Jules Bauer, *Notre enseignement religieux. Allocution prononcée à la distribution des cours d'instruction religieuse* (Nice, 1909).

Mention should be made of the following publications for school students: *La Vérité israélite*. Anthology of public religious instruction for the entire semester by the society of rabbis and men of letters. Editor: J. Cohen. Paris, No. 1, 19 January 1860, 24 pp. (—1863); *Le Foyer Israélite*. Supplement to *La Vérité israélite*. Paris, No. 1, 27 June 1861, 8 pp., 8° (—1863); *Le Foyer Israélite*. Journal of religious instruction appearing the first and third Saturday of each month, and published as a supplement devoted to Jewish youth, under the direction of Isaac Lévy, rabbi. Verdun, No. 1, January 1863, 6 pp. (1863–24 nos., 1864–12 nos.); *Supplément au No 1 du Foyer Israélite*, devoted to the instruction of young people. Verdun, No. 1, January 1863, 8 pp. (—1863–64); *Pour le Foyer—Pour l'Ecole*. Supplement to *L'Univers Israélite*. Paris, 1913-1914; *La Famille Israélite*. Supplement to *L'Univers Israélite*, Paris, 1 (18 April 1924), 8 pp. (—1926). It is also worthwhile to consult the *Freie Lehrer-und Kantoren Zeitung. Unabhängiges für die Interesser der Lehrer und Kantoren. Beilage* to the [Strassburg] *israelitischen Wochenschrift*, Strassburg, 1914-1915.

207. Reprinted from the Supplement to vol. 8 of *Jewish Social Studies* (1946) entitled, "Tentative List of Jewish Educational Institutions in Axis-Occupied Countries," prepared by the

Research Staff of the Commission on European Jewish Cultural Reconstruction, headed by Dr. Hannah Arendt.

The printed sources consulted then for this study include: J. Bauer, "L'Ecole Rabbinique," *REJ*, vols. 84, 85, and 88; *Annuaire des Archives Israélites pour 1926* (vol. 42); Tcherikower, *Yidn in Frankraykh* (New York, 1942); *Paix et Droit* (March 1931, June 1935, January 1939, March 1936, June 1932); *Bulletin de l'Alliance Israélite Universelle* (1911); A. H. Naon, *Les 70 ans de l'Ecole Normale Israélite Orientale: 1865–1935* (Paris, 1935); Narcisse Leven, *Cinquante ans d'histoire: l'Alliance Israélite Universelle: 1860–1910* (Paris, 1911), 2 vols.; Leon Berman, *Histoire des Juifs de France* (Paris, 1937); "ORT—Union. Extent of Its Vocational Training Work in Europe," mimeographed (Paris, 1940).

208. All figures are estimates; no official statistics are available.

209. Regarding the library, see the "Tentative List of Jewish Cultural Treasures in Axis-Occupied Countries," also a Supplement to *Jewish Social Studies*, 8 (January 1946).

INDEX OF NAMES

Aix, 58 n. 185

Alcan, Michel, 18

Algeria, 23, 27

Alliance Israélite Universelle, viii, xi, 14, 25, 28, 32; and teachers' training schools, 14, 23, 41-43

Alsace-Lorraine, Alsatian, 4-5, 7, 11, 18, 28; languages in, 19-20, 53 n. 124; population in, 1, 9, 19, 23, 27, 38; schools in, 3, 7, 20, 24, 34, 38, 41-42, 55 n. 159, re: curricula, 18, 53 n. 124, teachers, 10, 14, 21-23, 30, 48 n. 39; writers in, 5, 9, 23

Altkirch (Upper Rhine), 14, 50 n. 31

American Academy for Jewish Research, xii

American Jewish Joint Distribution Committee, xiii n. 2

Anchel, Robert, 3; as author, 46 n. 9

Arabic, 43

Army: American, vii; French, viii; Foreign Legion, vii, xiii n. 4

Archives Israélites, Les, 5, 7, 20, 22, 30, 32

Ashkenazim, 21, 24, 39

Association pour le développement de l'instruction elementaire et professionelle, 41

Astruc, Elie Aristide, 25, 29; as author, 54 ns. 150 and 153, 56 n. 163

Austria, 33, 40

Avignon, 2, 39, 58 n. 185

Bar Mitsvah preparation, 41, 44, 59-60 n. 189

Bayonne, 15, 30, 58 n. 185

Bédarride, Jassuda, 25; as author, 54 n. 150

Belfort, 58 n. 185

Belgium, xi, 17-18, 25, 27

Belleville district, 33

Benjamin, religious teacher, 8

Ben Tsaroth, hero of novel, 21

Bergheim, 47 n. 23

Berr, Berr Isaac, 9, 11, 22

Berr, Michel, 9, 29; as author, 47 n. 22, 48 n. 45

Besançon, 14, 58 n. 185

Bischheim, 7, 14, 27

Bischofsheim, 23

Bischofsheim Home for Jewish Girls, Paris, 23, 34

Bishop of Luçon, 28

Bloch, Joseph, 23, 57 n. 173; as author, 55 n. 159

Bloch, Maurice, 23; as author, 46 n. 13, 52 n. 112

Bloch, Moïse, 27; yeshivah, 24

Blum, Simon, 19

Bolshevism, x

Bordeaux, 17, 28; Consistory, 2, 4; population statistics, 38, 40; schools in, 1, 7, 10-11, 13-14, 30, 38, 47 n. 23, re: curricula, 20-21, 25, 49 n.

55, 58 n. 185, teachers, 22-23; Society for Propagation of Vocations among Jews, 4

Borokhov Yugnt, 36

Bouches-du-Rhône, 9

Boulogne, 58 n. 185

Brandeis University, xii

Braunschwig, Baruch, rabbi, 27

Brumath, 8

Bundists, vii, 36, 42; Workman's Circle, 36

Cahen, Isidore, 28; as author, 57 n. 174

Cahen, Samuel, 12, 19, 22, 30-31; Mrs. Samuel, 30

Carpentras, viii, 2, 30, 48 n. 1, 58 n. 185, 61 n. 206

Catholics and Catholicism, 28, 31-32; on conversion, 10, 28; on language, 21, 53 n. 124; in schools, 3-5, 8, 29, 31; in lay textbooks, 10, 24, 26

Central Europe, 1

Châlons-sur-Marne, 58 n. 185

Château-Salins, 10

Chevreuse, M., inspector, 20, 52 n. 118

Clermont, 58 n. 185

Cohen, Joseph, 15; as author, 51 n. 96

Cohn, Albert, 24, 29; as author, 56 n. 170, 59-60 n. 189

Colmar, 14, 19, 23, 28-29

Colonie Scolaire, 36

Comité des Dames, 44

Communists and Communism, vii, x; in schools, 21, 34, 36, 42; Communist Pioneers, 36; Communist Society of Friends of Yiddish Supplementary Schools (*Tsugabshuln*), 36, 42

Comtat Venaissin, viii, 39

Conseil d'Etat (State Council), 31

Considérant, Victor, 4

Consistories, 1, 5, 8, 17, 23, 27, 31-32, 35-37; Central, 2, 7, 17, 22, 24, 40, 43-44; on rabbinical schools, 3, 6, 27, 42; departmental: Bordeaux, 2, 4; Lower Rhine, 27; Marseilles, 4, 39; Metz, 14-15, 17; Nancy, 5, 7, 15; Paris, 3, 7, 11, 16, 21, 27, 30, 32, 34-35; Sainte Esprit-lès-Bayonne, 39; Upper Rhine, 27-28

Créhange, Alexandre Ben-Baruch, 10; as author, 48 n. 49, 50 n. 69, 54 n. 148, 56 n. 172, 59 n. 189

Crémieux, Adophe, 18-20; as author, 55 n. 159

Czyński, Jan, 20

Dalmbert, Simon Mayer, 4; as author, 46-47 n. 17

Dambach, 8

Darmeastater, James, 19

Derenbourg, Joseph, professor, 29
Deutsch, Emanuel, 21
Deutz, Emanuel, chief rabbi, 21
Dijon, 58 n. 185
Drach, David, 10, 12, 25
Dreyfus affair, viii, 39; Dreyfusards, 32
Dubnow, Simon, 25-26; as author, 54 n. 154
Dunkerque, 58 n. 185
Durmenach, 14, 47 n. 31
Dutlenheim, 23

Eastern Europe, vii, ix, 30, 34-37
Ecole(s): des Arts et Métiers (Strasbourg), 44; Ave-
    nue de Ségur (Paris), 34; le Chevalier (Paris), 24;
    Gustave de Rothschild (Paris), 35; Lucien de
    Hirsch (Paris), 34-35, 44; Louis le Grand (Paris),
    29, 56 n. 168; Maimonide, 29, 35, 43; Mater-
    nelles, 9; Normale (Marseilles), 4, 28; Normale
    Israélite Orientale (Paris), 43; Orientale Normale
    de Filles (Versailles), 43; Paris Talmud Torah,
    27; Petit Séminaire (Paris), 27; Place des Vosges
    (Paris), 24, 32; Rue Charlemagne Talmud Torah
    (Paris), 36; Rue des Hospitalières Saint Gervais
    (Paris), 32; Springer (Paris), 29, 56 n. 164; de
    Travail (Mulhouse), 44 and (Paris), 41, 43, pour
    Jeunes Filles (Institution Bischoffstein, Paris), 44;
    Zadoc Kahn (Paris), 13, 35. See also Rabbinical
    Seminary
Emancipation, Jewish, 2, 6-7, 9, 19-20, 30
Empire: First, 4; Second, ix
England, 10, 28
Ennery, Jonas, 18, 22; as author, 52 n. 112
Ennery, Marchand, chief rabbi, 18, 22
Epernay, 58 n. 185
Etendorf, 27
Expulsion of 1492, 25

Federation of Jewish Societies, 36, 42
Fegersheim, 8
Féret, 13
Franck, Adolphe, 24, 49-50 n. 67; as author, 57 n.
    173
Franco-Jewish school system, 11, 17-18, 25-26, 28,
    31, 35. See also Ecole(s)
Franco-Prussian War, 4
Frankfurt am Main, 12, 19
French (language), 20, 25, 32, 34-35
Fresco, David, 25; as author, 54 n. 154
Furtado, Abraham Auguste, mayor, 29

German-Jewish schools, 15, 29
German (language), 19-20, 25, 53 n. 124
Germany, viii-ix, xi, 1-2, 8, 11, 19, 24, 38, 40
Goudchaux, Michel, 18
Gradis family, 11; Benjamin, as author, 54 n. 147,
    55 n. 159; Eugenie-Rebecca Rodrigues Foa, as
    author, 55 n. 157
Greek (language), 25, 42
Grégoire, H., 2; as author, 46 n. 4
Grenoble, 40
Grussenheim, 47 n. 31

Hagenthal-le-Bas, 47 n. 31
Haguenau (Lower Rhine), 13, 28, 47 n. 23
Halévy, Léon, 18, 25; as author, 52 n. 113, 54 n.
    150
Halphen, A. Edmund, 15; as author, 46 n. 3
Haskalah (Enlightenment) movement, 2
Hatten, 8
Hebrew (language), 3, 19, 23, 30, 36; discouraged,
    12, 21; encouraged, 20, 22; in school curricula,
    20, 34-35; in textbooks, 24, 26. See also Yiddish
Hedarim, vi, 22, 36, 48 n. 39, 49 n. 55; number of,
    1, 8, 38, 40
Hegenheim, 14
Hellimer, 8
Hober, Samuel Jehuda, 21
Hochfelden, 8
Holocaust, viii, xi
Horbourg, 47 n. 31
Hourwitz, Zalkind, 2; as author, 46 n. 4
L'Humanité, 32
Hunczak, Taras, x
Hylan-Hillquit mayoralty contest, ix

Israel, xii
Italian (language), 25
Italy, 1

Jacobin, 24
Javal, Abraham, 29
Jérôme, Aron, 28
Jewish Book Council of America, xii; 1965 Leon Jol-
    son Award of, xiv n. 8
July Monarchy, 4, 6

Kahn, Léon, 2; as author, 45 n. 1
Kahn, Zadoc, 35; as author, 55 n. 159, 59 n. 188,
    59-60 n. 189
Kindergartens (asiles, salles d'asile, and écoles
    maternelles), 9
Kultur Lige, 36

Labor Zionists (Poale Zion), 36
Ladino (language), 25
Lambert, Lion Mayer, rabbi, 25; as author, 46 n.
    5, 54 n. 150, 59-60 n. 189
Lambert, Mayer, 17; as author, 58 n. 181
Latin, 43
Lauterbourg, 8
League for Human Rights, 32-33
Léon, Isidore, 30
Lévi-Alvarès, David, 18
Lévy, Emile, rabbi, 39; as author, 53 n. 132, 58 n.
    180
Lévy, Gerson, 15; as author, 51 n. 94, 60 n. 200
Liber, Maurice, rabbi, 12
Lille, 28, 40, 58 n. 185
London, 12; Whitechapel section in, 10
Louvigny, 10
Lower Rhine, 18, 22; Consistory, 39; educational
    statistics, 7, 13, 27, 38
Lunéville, 14, 28, 52 n. 113

Luther, Martin, 24
Lycées, 11–12, 21, 28–30, 56 n. 168. *See also* Ecole(s), Franco-Jewish school system and Schools, Christian
Lyon(s), 39–40, 58 n. 185, 61 n. 206

Maas, Jewish teacher, 24
Magnes, Judah, x
Manuel, Eugène, 18–19, 28, 30, 33; as author, 53 n. 121, 56 n. 162
Marseilles, 2, 5, 13, 17, 24, 30; Consistory, 4, 39; educational statistics, 40, 42, 47 ns. 19 and 23, 58 n. 185
Marx, Edgar, 4
Marx, L., rabbi, 29; as author, 57 n. 173
Metz, 1–2, 9, 17, 24; Consistory, 14–15, 17; schools in, re: curricula, 19–20, 22; early education, 5, 8–9, 44; Rabbinical Academy (later Ecole Rabbinique in Paris), 2, 11, 27, 56 n. 171, statistics, 13–15, 27, 30, 40; vocational training, 15–16, 23. *See also* Rabbinical Seminary
Meyer, Lévi, rabbi, 16
Meyer, Maurice, 31; as author, 51 n. 95
Ministry of Education, 4, 7, 41, 43
Montmartre, 35
Montpellier, 14
Moselle, department of, 2–3, 14, 38
Moutzig, 23
Mulhouse, 5, 19, 30, 44, 48 n. 44
Munk, Salomon, 24
Mutuelle method (teachers' aides), 4, 22

Nancy, 3, 18, 22, 50 n. 67; Consistory, 5, 7, 15; schools in, re: curricula, 29, 58 n. 185; early education, 5, 7, 13–14, 30, 47 n. 23; educational statistics, 16, 40
Nantes, 3, 58 n. 185
Napoléon: I, vii–ix; fall of his regime, 4; III, 18
Nathan, J. M., rabbi, 23
Nazism, x
Nice, 58 n. 185
Nîmes, 39, 58 n. 185, 61 n. 206
North African Jews, viii, 36

Oath, "More Judaico," 1
"Ohel Jacob" community, 21, 53 n. 131
Orange, 58 n. 185
Orthodox and Orthodoxy, 10, 21, 29, 42; conflicts with Reform, 8, 17–18, 27, 31; other conflicts, 19, 24, 34

Palestine, 21
Paris, vi, 2, 6, 9–10, 17, 29; languages used in, 19–21, 30, 35; schools in, re: curricula, 20–21, 25, 30; early education, 1, 8–9, 17, 29, 47 n. 23; financing of, 7, 13–14, 22; lycées, 11–12; proposals for, 3–6, 11, 23, 29, 33; Rabbinical Seminary, 42–43; statistics, 8, 12, 18, 30, 34–36, 40, 58 ns. 181 and 185. *See also* Ecole(s). Societies in, 27, 31–32; vocational training in, 16, 23. *See also* Consistories

Petliura, Symon, x
Peyrehorade, 22, 39
Poale Zion (Labor Zionists), 36, 42
Polack, L., teacher, 22; as author, 53 n. 132
Poznański, Samuel, vi
Protestants and Protestantism, 10, 20, 28, 31; in schools, 3–4, 8, 13–14, 22, 47 n. 19
Provençe, 3, 20

Raba family, 11
Rabbinical Seminary of Paris, 27, 29, 41–43. *See also* Ecole(s) and Metz
Reform Jews, 7, 19, 25; conflicts with Orthodox, 8, 17–18, 27, 31
Régénération, La, 19, 23
Reguisheim, 47 n. 31
Reims, 58 n. 185
Reign of Terror, 2
Reinach, Théodore, 21, 25
Revolutions: vi, ix; Bolshevik, x; French, 1–3, 18; of 1830, 6, 28; of 1848, 18, 28, 31; Russian of 1905, x
Ribeauvilliers, 47 n. 23
Rimbach (Upper Rhine), 3
Rishon Le-Zion, 21
Rixheim, 47 n. 31
Rodrigues, Olinde, 28
Rome, 28
Root, Elihu, x
Rosenfeld, Jules, 29, 57 n. 173
Rothschild family, 40–41; Mrs. Robert de, 41, 44. *See also* Ecole(s)
Royal Commission for Education, 8
Royal Council of Public Education (*Conseil royal de l'instruction publique*), 5
Rumania, ix, 34, 40
Russia-Poland, vi–vii, x–xii, xiii n. 2, 34, 40

Saint-Esprit-lès-Bayonne, 2, 8–9, 29–30, 39
Saint-Etienne, 28–29, 58 n. 185, 61 n. 206
Saint-Quentin, 58 n. 185
Saint Simonians, xiv n. 7, 15, 18, 28
Salvador, Joseph, 19
Sarcey, Francisque, 33
Sarchi, Filippo, 24; as author, 54 n. 145
Sarrebourg, 14
Sarreguemines, 14, 47 n. 23
Saverne (Lower Rhine), 3
Schools: Christian, 10, 12; Jewish, *see also* Ecole(s) and Franco-Jewish school system
Schwab, Moïse, 25; as author, 54 n. 150
Second Temple, destruction of, 25
Sedan, 58 n. 185
Sélestat, 19–20
Seligman, Michel, rabbi, 21
Separation of Church and state, 11, 31–34, 39, 43, 58 n. 181
Sephardim, viii–ix, 20, 22, 25, 29–30, 36, 39
Servedier, Abelard, professor, 28
Sierentz, 18, 27, 47 ns. 23 and 31
Simon, Jules, minister of education, 18

Singer, David, 17; as author, 47 n. 23
Skif (of the Bund), 36
Socialists, ix, xiv n. 7, 32–33
Société des bons livres de Strasbourg, 24
Société israélite des livres moraux et religieux (Hevrah Thora V'emuna), 24
Soultzmatt, 27, 47 n. 31
Spanish (language), 43
Stauben, Daniel, 23; as author, 53–54 n. 137
Strasbourg, 18, 22, 24, 28; schools in, 4–5, 8, 10, 19, 30, 42, 44, 47 n. 23; and statistics, 14, 38, 40
Switzerland, 27
Szajkowski, Zosa (Yehoshua Frydmann), bibliography of, vi–xiv n. 5; biography of, vi–viii, xi–xiii ns. 1 and 4, xiv n. 6

Tcherikower, Elias, vii–viii; Rivka, vii
Thann, 47 n. 31
Thermidorian reaction (1794), 2
Thiery, A., 2; as author, 46 n. 4
Thionville, 47 n. 23
Toul, 14, 58 n. 185
Toulouse, 39–40, 58 n. 185
Tsarphati (Olry Terquem), 9, 17; as author, 48 n. 45, 53 n. 125, 55 n. 158
Tsugabshuln (supplementary schools), 36, 40, 42

Ulmann, Salomon, chief rabbi, 24–25; as author, 46 n. 5, 47 n. 22, 54 n. 148, 55 n. 158
Ulmo, Jacob, rabbi, 27
L'Union Scolaire, 31
United States, viii–x, xii
L'Univers Israélite, 12, 28, 34, 61 n. 206
Upper Rhine department, 3, 5, 7, 9–10, 13–14, 27–28, 38. *See also* Consistories

Valabrègue, Elias, 30
Valenciennes, 58 n. 185
Vaucluse, department of, 39
Vendée, 28
Versailles Peace Conference, xi
Vesoul, 58 n. 185
Vitry, 58 n. 185
Voltaire (François Marie Arouet), 23

Walentheim, 10
Warsaw, vi, xiii n. 2; Training Seminary for Teachers of the Jewish Faith, vi
Weill, professor of mathematics, 28
Weill, Alexandre, 12, 19; as author, 48 n. 39, 52 n. 114, 53 n. 133
Weill, Jacques, 18; as author, 52 n. 113
Werth, Léon, 18
Westhoffen, 27
Wintzenheim, 5, 27
Wissembourg, 24
World War: I, vi, ix–xi; II, vii–viii, xi, 36, 54 n. 143

Yiddish, vi–viii, 22, 25; in curriculum, 19, 21–22, 35, 42; discouraged, 19–21, 32; supplementary schools (*Tsugabshuln*), 36, 42. *See also* Hebrew
YIVO Institute for Jewish Research, New York (formerly YIVO-Yiddish Scientific Institute, Wilno), vii–viii; *Bleter*, viii; librarian, xiii n. 1; = Yad Vashem project, viii
Yom Kippur, 14

Zaręby Kościelne (Zaromb), vi, xi, xiii n. 2
Zay, Lazare, 24
Zionists and Zionism, xi, 26, 36–37, 40